# GOLI OTOK
Hell in the Adriatic

Josip Zoretić

## Pronunciation Guide

| Letter | Pronunciation |
| --- | --- |
| c | like **ts** in le**ts** |
| č (hard) | like **ch** in **ch**urch |
| ć (soft) | like **ch** in **ch**eese |
| đ | like **j** in **j**eep |
| lj | like **lli** in mi**lli**on |
| š | like **sh** in **sh**ip |
| ž | like **s** in mea**s**ure |

*All rights reserved.*

First published 1972 in Croatian
© 1972
English translations © 2002-2004
Forward copyright © 2004 by Ivana Cota
© 2002-2007

"Goli Otok," by Josip Zoretić. ISBN 978-1-58939-990-7.

Library of Congress Control Number: 2007923027.

Published 2007 by Virtualbookworm.com Publishing Inc., P.O. Box 9949, College Station, TX 77842, US. ©2007, Josip Zoretić. All rights reserved. No part of this publication may be reproduced, stored in a retrieval system, or transmitted in any form or by any means, electronic, mechanical, recording or otherwise, without the prior written permission of Josip Zoretić.

Manufactured in the United States of America.

*Josip Zoretić*

# Foreword

## by Ivana Cota
Original English translation

Every summer thousands of tourists from all over Europe and the world flock to the Adriatic coast of Croatia. Once they arrive, they often go on one day boat ride excursions to nearby historical sites, beautiful beaches and islands. The choices are abundant, and on the northern Croatian coast there is one place that is increasingly found on itineraries. That place is Goli Otok, pronounced "go-lee o-toke," which means bare or naked island. Unfortunately, its recent popularity is for reasons other than being situated along the beautiful Adriatic coast.

Goli Otok is not a romantic place. It is an uninhabited and almost completely barren island. In the summer it is hot, with temperatures of 35-40 degrees Celsius, while in the winter it is subject to the chilling Bura wind. In other words, Goli Otok is the perfect place for a nation to send those they wish to remove from society. That is exactly what the Yugoslav government did when there was a Yugoslavia, with Croatia as one of its republics.

A heavy labor prison was set up for a spectrum of inmates, from cold-blooded murderers to the communist regime's most hated and feared enemies – its political prisoners. It was a prison from which it was almost impossible to escape, and a prison where many people disappeared from the light of day and darkness of night, without a word to their families. The treatment of the convicts was inhuman and akin to the treatment of prisoners in German concentration camps of World War Two. What happened on Goli Otok, however, occurred during times of peace.

The reasons that brought Josip Zoretić to Goli Otok were just as absurd as the things he had to endure. A ridiculous case against him and a more ridiculous trial resembling Kafka's fiction, only this was very much real. The sentence pronounced – seven years in a maximum security prison – was almost a death sentence, for even if one did manage to stay alive for so long on Goli Otok, one was almost sure to go insane. But he chose to survive in spite of the injustice, the torture, and the regime; and he has the courage to tell his story, which, sadly, is the story of many others who didn't survive or haven't had the strength to tell it themselves.

I don't suppose there is a single reader who will not be struck deeply by the contents of this book. The gloomy atmosphere, physical and mental torture, and helplessness described are so disturbing that they kept me awake at night after I worked on its translation. I then read the final few sentences, which struck me even more – the worst things that happened haven't even been described. It is certainly understandable that he wishes to keep that to himself, for the obvious reason that he wishes to forget them and get on with his life, although I doubt he ever will forget.

*Goli Otok* is more than just a book and more than just a biography; it is a historical document of a shameful past. History, as we all know, tends to repeat itself, and it does so because we learn so little from it. Unlike the author, we must not try to forget. Let us hope that enough people will hear this story and finally learn a lesson that is so important – never forget and never let it happen again!

*Josip Zoretić*

# Introduction

Upon my arrival to Canada in September 1970, I promised myself to write this book and to share my story. Yet, I am desperate to forget the misdeeds I endured. To forget would quell my nightmares, bring trust to my relationships, and heal. Heal what they did to me and to so many others from my native soil. The absurdity of what I endured causes me to have moments of disbelief. As I write this and think back, I sometimes wonder, could something like this have actually occurred? The conclusion is, unfortunately, inescapable.

For reasons that I will later explain, in 1962 I fled communist Yugoslavia and went to Austria. However, only a few kilometers into Austria, near the border city of Šentilj, I became ill and turned myself in to the Austrian police who deported me back to Yugoslavia.

After returning to Yugoslavia and spending a month in custody I was released and free until August 22, 1962. That was when I was again arrested, along with many others. We were arrested by members of the Yugoslav Police Interior Department on charges of being "anti-state elements" and opponents of the regime. In that year alone 13,000 Croats, 3,700 Albanians, 1,700 Slovenes, 1,200 Bosnian Muslims, several hundred Serbs, and a small number of other national minorities living in Yugoslavia such as Italians, Hungarians and Bulgarians, among others, were imprisoned.

This is how I, along with many others, got to the infamous Goli Otok, literally meaning "naked island" – a heavy labor correctional institution on an island in the Adriatic. This is where I unjustly suffered seven years as a victim with the rest of the so-called members of the anti-state regime.

This book is a testament to the atrocities that were committed on this island measuring only 4.7 square kilometers. An island with no fresh water, no grass or any sort of vegetation. All that was there were bare rocks, the special police, in winter the Bura – an unpredictable cold north-easterly wind blowing from the mainland toward the sea in gusts up to 120 kilometers per hour – and in the summer the heat that rose to 40 degrees Celsius.

The misdeeds that exceeded those in Hitler's concentration camps happened on Goli Otok and have never been officially recorded. But they happened on this bare island, partly because its geographical position enabled it. It is situated between the island of Rab and the foot of the Velebit Mountain range, the mainland being over two kilometers away across the Senj Channel in the Adriatic Sea off the coast of Croatia.

The torture I saw and endured will not remain a secret of the Yugoslav bloodthirsty butchers, psychopaths and savages who took great pleasure in giving in to their sadistic impulses on this desolate island. I write this book not for myself, as it can't change anything for me, but for those who can't tell their story. These are the true events of the horrors of Goli Otok from 1962-1969.

*Josip Zoretić*

# Youth and Circumstance

*Man is not the creature of circumstances.*
*Circumstances are the creatures of men.*
              Benjamin Disraeli


To tell this story, I have to start at the beginning. Seeing my childhood friends, whose fathers were alive in 1945 after the war, enjoying their freedom and lives, forced me, an eight-year-old, to ask my mother where my father was. My mother often answered my frequent questions by saying, "Oh my son, don't break my already broken heart even more!" One day I asked my mother the same old question again. She relented and answered that the reason why she was alone with no help from anyone or anything was that in 1942 the Partisans took my father away and threw him into a mass grave in Sošice, Žumberak, near the Croatian-Slovenian border, because he refused to join their army. My mother was left to fend for herself and her seven children, the oldest my twelve-year-old sister and the youngest my brother who was only four months old.

I later found out that the mass grave in Sošice was not a traditional mass grave, if there is such a thing. Thousands of people were executed at Sošice during WWII, forced down a hole in the ground, dead or alive, into a cavernous pit 43 meters deep and 17 meters wide near the bottom. It is rumored that one Croatian prisoner with his hands tied bit his executioner's ankle and managed to pull him down with him.

Those who kept disposing of prisoners were surprised that the hole, which was only a meter in diameter at the top, never filled up. Bodies stopped being thrown down only when local villagers complained about the presence of blood in the local stream water. Today, a mound of skeletal remains is still there – many with holes in their skulls and skeletal hands bound with wire.

This is where my father lies.

I barely remember the man that was my father, much less know who he was. Through people that knew him, I discovered that he was a gentle, intelligent, educated and just man. He did not believe in neither communism nor fascism. As extremes, he felt these forces were inherently wrong and did not support either view as the best option for the Croatian people. But, as the old saying in the region went, "you are either with us or against us." My father's refusal to join the communist Partisans was his demise. Little did he know that not only would he pay the ultimate price for his beliefs, but his children would suffer more than the loss of a father.

When WWII ended the Croatians weren't free. The Yugoslav communists continued repressing and haunting all progressive forces as anti-state elements. All those who in any way showed signs of concern or displeasure with the communists were put away and silenced.

The children of murdered parents from the "wrong side" were denied proper access to elementary schooling, not to mention higher levels of education. We were also denied jobs, including the most basic ones. My siblings and I were guilty by association – punished for the sins of our father by his refusing to join the communist Partisans. We were labeled anti-state elements and fascists.

Enduring this for years yet hoping to see better days, I stayed in Yugoslavia and tried to live a regular life. Due to the military service's ineffective control I was even admitted to a military officer school. But this did not last. I was subsequently discharged after only four months once knowledge of my father was realized.

At one point I even volunteered to work on the Highway of Brotherhood and Unity, hoping that the regime would see me as a "good boy" and give me a job somewhere else. They accepted my volunteer work, but it proved fruitless as I was again treated no differently than before.

I couldn't continue to live this way. As many other people in this world do, I yearned for freedom and the opportunity for a normal life; but I couldn't simply gather my things and take the next train out of the country. Just like the Eastern Communist Block countries, we were prisoners in our homeland and weren't free to leave on our own volition if we weren't Communist Party Members. At that time, only those who could present their Party Membership books could be issued passports. I, along with every member of my family and many Croatians, were never permitted to receive Party Membership, nor did we particularly care to have it.

Realizing the desperate and hopeless situation I was in, I was forced to go through with the most drastic plan and attempt an escape from Yugoslavia, even though I was aware of the consequences of a potential failure.

In the region around my home village of Sršići there were rumors that others wanted to escape as well. These rumors were true and six acquaintances of mine, all having lost their fathers in the same way, planned to escape together.

In 1962 we illegally escaped across the

border into Austria, intending to make it as far into Austria as we could and hopefully into Germany – the farther away from Yugoslavia the better. But we never made it further than Graz, a town in Austria close to the Slovenian border.

The shoes I was wearing were old and uncomfortable and caused me to develop excruciating blisters. I attempted to continue on in my bare feet but the sections of railroad tracks I walked along tore them up even further and they began to bleed. We were all in bad shape and had no choice but to turn ourselves in to the Austrian authorities, which we did.

We were sent to a camp with other refugees from Eastern Europe with hardly a question asked of us. I felt there was a 50/50 chance that I would be forced to return to Yugoslavia. The Austrian authorities attempted to have me treated at the camp, but it was suggested by the person in charge that the treatment would be better carried out in Yugoslavia. In my opinion, *no treatment* was better than any form of "treatment" I would receive in Yugoslavia.

I was one of the unlucky ones. Two weeks later my name was called out to board a bus and I was delivered to the Yugoslav authorities on the Spillfeld-Šentilj border crossing near the Slovenian town of Maribor. The names of the others I escaped with weren't called and I never saw them again.

We were thrown into the Radgona collection camp near Maribor with others who were being returned from Austria and Italy. We were received with words such as *Bastards! We'll show you what becomes you, you traitors! Empty your pockets!*

There were several Slovenian police officers mocking and threatening us.

I was there for four days when a bus with Belgrade license plates followed by a convoy of other buses arrived. Upon their arrival it was forbidden for anyone to speak Slovenian because of the presence of non-Slovenes. The bus and convoy were sent at the direction of Tito's Minister of the Interior, the Secret Police Chief, Aleksander Ranković.

Ranković was bent on creating or transforming Yugoslavia into a Greater Serbia. In order to achieve his goal Ranković appointed as many pure Serbs as possible to posts in the police and had increased the number of public safety troop members (the militia) and orchestrated the mass arrests of the Croats, Slovenes and Albanians under the pretense that they had weapons, that they were spreading anti-state policy, and working on the destruction of Yugoslavia. This ethnic and political persecution was done without any evidence, but it didn't matter, since the judiciary was under Ranković's direct influence. Sentences of two to fifteen years were imposed.

Some time later the arrests were extended to other nationalities: Macedonians, Montenegrins, Hungarians and a smaller portion of Serbs. Arresting the Serbs was but a disguise technique; it enabled Ranković to keep his plan a mystery. This plan was secretly financed by managers of various firms and institutions, all of them pure Serbs of course, some of whom were later exposed and sentenced.

Ranković's persecution extended with even greater ferocity to those who were repatriated. He had ordered the takeover of the deported persons center near Maribor from the Slovene republican authorities to Belgrade, considering the Slovenes traitors. From there he personally directed the handling of the so-called "returnees," designating many as organizers of actions to overthrow the government. Even though the returnees were mostly non-political émigrés, Ranković used these bogus grounds to carry out among them a "suspicious persons" arresting campaign. Croats and Slovenes were arrested more often than others because these nations were allegedly still determined to oppose the dictatorship coming from the Serbs and their friends from the USSR.

A group of us, all Croats, was transported by bus from the Radgona camp to a prison at the Croatian town of Šišljavić. I was there for two weeks when a paddy wagon came to transport me to Zagreb.

I was the only prisoner in the wagon. Beside the driver was a police officer. I was handcuffed in the back with a police officer on each side of me.

Not long into the trip and without provocation the police officers in the back began beating me and repeatedly hit me as hard as they could beneath my ribs and at my kidneys.

I was in bad shape, heavily coughing and spitting up blood, when we arrived at the police station in Zagreb. For some reason unknown to me a colonel and two military police officers were present at the station. Upon seeing me, the colonel told the police that they had to let me go because I was in such bad shape that he was afraid I was going to die there and he didn't want to explain my death.

They released me right away.

Having no place else to go and still with enough money for a train ticket, I made my way back to my home village, Sršići. Of course, I didn't die as they thought I might.

After a few days to recover, I decided to go to Ljubljana and stayed at a friend's house in the hope of finding work, since the Slovenians were more willing to employ me than my fellow Croatians. After about a week I managed to find a job as a bricklayer. Unfortunately, it wouldn't last.

*Goli Otok*

## Torture

*It is better by noble boldness to run the risk of being subject to half of the evils we anticipate than to remain in cowardly listlessness for fear of what might happen.*
                                        Herodotus


After less than a month in Ljubljana I was arrested on August 22, 1962 by the Ljubljana police. They stressed that it wasn't their idea and not to be upset with them – they had received orders from the military in Zagreb to arrest me. They treated me humanely and on August 24 I was transferred from Ljubljana to the Zagreb military court on Nova Ves Street. You couldn't tell from the outside what the building was and the locals didn't even know that it housed a military court and prison.

I was completely clueless as to what was going to become of me, especially after being put into solitary. Half an hour after I was confined Comrade Popov, a lieutenant-colonel in civilian clothes, came to my cell and said to me ironically:

"How are you, birdie? You've been at large, flying around for a long time, but here you are in our cage."

"I don't know you" I said, "and I have no idea what birdie you're talking about."

"Shut up you treacherous scum! The Austrians have trained you well, but you'll start talking shortly. This here is a decree about opening proceedings against you and maybe later against others!"

He then slammed the door and the prison guard bolted it three times.

The interrogation started later that same day, run by a whole apparatus of Ranković's servants working in the military prison in Zagreb.

"Listen to me, you asshole; tell us everything you know or else you'll get the worst of it. We know everything! We just want to make sure you're honest."

"I don't know what all this is about or why I was arrested in the first place."

"Don't you start acting now, blockhead! Smartass! I'll prove to you that we know everything, but you'd better start talking on your own. If I start talking first, you will face your doom."

"What the hell are you begging him for?" shouted Lieutenant-Colonel Prodanović. "I don't even want to touch this shit. Take him downstairs! And let us know when you've thought this through and then we'll talk again."

"Don't you turn around, just walk straight towards the basement, do you hear what I'm saying?" said the guard.

I gathered from his accent that he could be from around the city of Niš, Serbia.

"What, for God's sake, have you done? You see the whole place is full, you're not alone, and you're only making trouble. We have to keep an eye on you and guard you twenty-four hours a day, and you fools don't get it! Well, cool off in here and you'll come to your senses. When you want to confess everything just bang on the door and I'll take you back upstairs."

He bolted the door and left.

Fifteen days passed in this dark cage and I didn't bang on the door.

## Goli Otok

Popov was less patient than I was so he sent for me.

"Here is the indictment issued by the military prosecution against you on the grounds of the information they got from the authorities."

Political and nationalistic hostility and disputes were still noticeably present in the area where I was born. By giving information about others to the authorities and acting as informants, the people there tried to appear as patriots. To make the situation more precarious, some were members of Ranković's secret service. The area I'm referring to, a part of Žumberak near the Slovenian border, is largely inhabited by the Serbs called *Vlahi*, mortal enemies of the Croats and Slovenes. By living so close to the Croatian population they had a wonderful opportunity of undermining the Croatian people on Croatian territory, which they did as much as they could. In the Karlovac district, separation of Croatians and Serbs was taking place, and Croats started to lose their jobs because they opposed Tito's regime during the war. Belgrade supported the Serbs and didn't allow any changes in the commanding apparatus in the Karlovac district. Orders were issued to arrest people for trifles and to close cases quickly, which was how it had always been done since 1945.

Popov changed his interrogation methods.

"Get talking! You know nothing, do you? You don't have to say anything now; you'll start talking in the end, but by that time it'll be too late!" he said while he was nervously pacing up and down his office.

"Not answering my questions means confirming everything I say. Maybe you'll talk when you're back in your cell. Let's go downstairs!"

He called a guard and we descended the stairs toward the basement. The guard opened the door and pointed to my cell; Popov then asked to see Lieutenant-Colonel Prodanović and dismissed the guard.

"Why do you need me?" I heard a voice say a few moments later. His presence was necessary, said Popov, and then he asked me: "Well, are you going to talk or not?"

"I have nothing to say!"

"Is that right? Many have said this before, but they all talked in the end. So don't waste anymore time and start talking, you traitor!"

Several seconds later I found myself lying on the floor. I was hit in the stomach and didn't even notice it until I was down. I was hit some more with kicks to my ribs.

Prodanović helped me up.

The blows weren't all that bad because he was wearing civilian shoes with crepe-rubber soles. Making it through this, I later found, was a piece of cake!

"It's up to you to decide whether we're going to watch a movie. Call the head of security!"

He arrived shortly.

"Tie this bastard against the wall and let him stay like that till I'm back!"

"Yes, Comrade Lieutenant-Colonel."

He appeared with a big rough chain with a lock and said: "Tie him up real tight and don't let anybody come near him until I'm back!"

The concrete walls were so cold I thought they were made of ice. It also felt as if I was there for ages. There were no windows in the dugout cell. One cellar after another. You couldn't even hear the strikes from the clock tower of the Zagreb cathedral nearby. Day or night, it was all the same down there.

While pondering my predicament I heard a voice and a few seconds later I heard the door open. Three men stood in the doorway and pointed their flashlights at me.

"Look at him, he's sleepy," said one of them.

"Well, you bum, should we take you upstairs if you've decided to confirm the truth, so we can stop trying to get you to talk?"

"I know nothing."

"Yeah, right, now you know nothing. Okay, it's 1 a.m., untie him and let him rest for tomorrow morning. He's still young and stupid and likes to joke around, right? Why not? He could make an excellent actor, don't you think so, Pero? He's so good at acting, but still stupid – he doesn't realize there are no cameras around. Too bad a talent like this is going to waste in here of all places, ha, ha, ha! He's a clever little canary, but he doesn't like this cage. Not for now, but he'll get used to it soon enough. He's not worth our wasting time on him."

An airforce captain, whose rank I was able to read by the reflections of the flashlight, said: "You're right, we haven't lost anything by coming here. We just stopped by on our way back from a night out. You'd better think about this! You have time until tomorrow to start singing!"

They left and closed the door behind them.

Nobody came to my cell the next day. At night the cook came in the same way as the officers did the night before, and said: "There, here's something for you, but this is all you're going to get because you're not registered as a food recipient."

"It's a waste to give him even this much. It would be better to throw it away than feed the bandits!" said the assistant warden, a captain.

"You should all be killed, you traitors! Too bad I don't make the laws so I could finally get to the truth and find out who's who and what's what!"

He shut the door and left.

Later in the night Popov appeared again with two other men and said he had been fair and had already given me more time to think than necessary. He asked if I had changed my mind.

"I couldn't possibly change my mind!"

"Is that so? Fine! He needs a good bashing. Let's start with a blow to the stomach, then to his groin, then a heavy blow or two to his ears!"

And so they did.

"Watch the top actor theatrically fall on the floor! I hope we haven't misjudged him. But I've been dealing with this kind of petty scum for years and I know them all too well."

I was hit a few more times in the ribs near my liver and then I fainted. It was real agony. I was bathed in sweat when I came to.

"I told you he was an excellent actor. You see, he's quite alright! Let's entertain him a bit! Jovo, set up a swing for him like you did before, but let's add something to it this time."

This so-called Jovo fastened a chain on an iron ring that was attached to the ceiling and a piece of wooden plank was then secured to the pendant part of the chain. My hands were then tied behind my back and my legs fixed to the chain. I was then lifted to hang upside down, just an inch or two above the floor. I couldn't move at all. Comrade Popov made a special strap with which he fixed me to the chain under my armpits so that I couldn't possibly change my position while hanging on this communist swing.

"There's your branch, birdie! You just sit here and we'll come to visit you as soon as we get the chance!" They then left.

Hanging like that I felt the blood in my legs stop circulating. I was trying so hard to touch the floor, but with all my efforts I couldn't do it. I was always an inch or two too far up. By the time it got dark I felt I could make it with no problem, but after about sixteen hours I really couldn't feel my legs at all. But then Ranković's men came and lowered me down on the floor. No use – my legs wouldn't keep me standing.

"Ha, ha, ha, look at the softy! The act is as good as ever. Lets go and let him think!"

The food I was given from now on was on a regular basis and similar to what the army was getting. But it was the speed of eating required that forced me to swallow without chewing. I had only three minutes to eat before the cook and guard returned to take it away.

For six days nobody entered my cell except when food was brought in. On the seventh day the commanding guard officer came and told me to get ready for further questioning.

As I didn't cooperate with the makers of Greater Serbia that time either, I was transferred to another cell. This one was more modern, with a wooden floor and a tiny window facing the court hallway. This was my abode for the next twenty-or-so days. I was questioned a few times, only now I wasn't beaten.

Soon things got worse again. I was transferred to yet another cell, and again different methods of interrogation were applied.

"Do we have to force you to talk? That's fine with us, we've got time!"

"There's nothing to talk about!" I said.

Three lieutenant-colonels and a major were there. They tied up my arms and legs, put my fingers between the door and the door-post and squeezed them just hard enough to inflict terrible pain but not hard enough to break any bones. After several hours of tormenting they went back upstairs. They untied my arms before they left, but soon enough they were so swollen that I had no use of them.

The interrogation continued without anymore bashing, but I could still feel a sharp pain in my liver. It caused me to squeeze my teeth from time to time, which Popov noticed.

"What is it, squeezing your teeth out of anger, are you? It's not my fault that you have no brains. You could have spared yourself this trouble; you've seen it's no use being stubborn. Can't you see that?"

He threw a file folder in front of me and continued.

"These are the statements made by one of your aldermen, by the militia station chief, and by many others. I'm just telling you this so that you know that we know everything. But this is not enough. We want you to tell us the truth and get it over with. You're young, inexperienced, maybe seduced, and that's exactly why nothing can happen to you if you're honest. Just say where you got the money that you used for going to Austria and Italy and who else is in this with you. You see, we know you're not alone in this. You don't have to tell us, but you're screwed if we find something out later!"

"It is true that I spent some time in Italy. I had saved some money while working. I was in

Austria as a refugee, not as a tourist!"

"Why did you return from Austria then if Yugoslavia wasn't good enough for you?"

"I became sick and the Austrian authorities had me deported because of my condition."

"Don't you lie to me! You Croats and Slovenes keep wanting Vienna to be your capital instead of Belgrade, and you keep forgetting the million and seven hundred thousand victims we sacrificed for what we have today! You tell me the truth now! Why did the Austrians send you back and who else is working with you, or . . . ? What have you been telling them?"

"They're not interested in your depots, high-ranking officers or weapons. Nobody asked me about that!"

"Not another word! I can tell that you're lying! I've got plenty of time, I'm going on a vacation and you are going to wait until I get back."

And I did wait. Fifteen days later the vacation was over and the interrogation continued.

"Let's not play anymore games, why don't you start talking?"

"I have nothing to tell you," I answered.

"Fine. Guard, take him back to his cell!"

The night came and some time around midnight the same old group of officers visited me and continued the torture but now used a new method. They took me to the same dark cell as before and tied me up against the wall which had already been prepared for torturing. They spread my arms and legs open, secured them firmly in the irons embedded into the wall, and pushed toothpicks under my fingernails and toenails. They did it slowly so that by the end there wasn't a drop of sweat left in my body. They were all furious with me for not talking, especially the chief of investigation, Popov.

"You fucking son of a bitch! You'll talk in the end!"

But they didn't get what they wanted.

I remained in this room for two days after the torturing session and then I was called to a hearing again, but I didn't utter a word.

"Take him downstairs," ordered Popov.

Another night came, another torturing session, but this time without bashing. Instead, they shaved some hair from the top of my head and let water drip on the shaven area. It didn't seem unbearable at first, but after about an hour it seemed like it had drilled a hole from the top of my head all the way down to my chin.

My liver was in a bad state, my arms and legs were no better, and on top of all that I had developed high fever.

The next morning the same officers came again, and again they pushed toothpicks under my nails.

I had now reached the limit of what I was able to endure and I suffered a nervous breakdown.

I woke up in a bed, my mouth full of blisters, my lips all bitten and bloody, my arms and legs swollen, and my sputum brown. I found out later that their doctor came to see me.

After about ten days I signed everything that Popov wanted me to sign.

*Goli Otok*

# "Trial"

*We know that if one man's rights are denied, the rights of all are endangered.*
Robert F. Kennedy


The trial against me began – the court created by the imaginary work of Aleksandar Ranković.

Present at the trial were five judges, all wearing their military uniforms: Chairman of the Court Lieutenant-Colonel Kapetanovic, who had a noticeable leg injury, Lieutenant-Colonel Janez Trost, Colonel Plačić and two majors whose names I didn't know. Also present were the military prosecutor Colonel Smoljanović, the defense representative Lieutenant-Colonel Grujo Čurgus, court reporter Špedieri (no rank), and several other officers.

There were no cameras. It was a military court, even though I wasn't in the military, and I wasn't permitted to have a civilian lawyer.

The judges sat facing me from behind their bench. I sat on a bench in the middle of the room. In front of me to the left was Colonel Smoljanović's desk. He didn't use the desk much – instead choosing to walk around while he talked. Lieutenant-Colonel Čurgus sat in a chair near me.

The process started with the following words from Kapetanovic: "Comrades present, as well as the defendant, I hereby inform you that anything that is discussed here must under no circumstances be discussed among civilians. Should it be proven that somebody has spoken about this trial, that person shall be punished with a minimum of five years in a maximum security prison.

Has the defendant understood the explanation?"
"I have."
"Let us then continue with the evidence signed by the defendant himself, which in turn means that he has admitted to being guilty of the criminal offense of espionage as described in Article 105, Subsections 1 and 2. I am asking the court to take a good look at the indictment, and ask that the defendant be punished severely according to law. Let us first confirm the defendant's personal data. Parents: Marko and Katarina born Strehan, place of birth . . . is the data correct? Are your parents still living and what do they do?"
"My mother is a housewife and my father manures the land."
"What do you mean he manures the land? Is he a forester or does he work in a nursery-garden or what?"
"Neither. You know very well where he is. You know that your current General-Colonel Milan Žeželj had him disposed of in 1942, so the land is growing on him and he is its manure."
Chairman of the court then stood up and suggested a short break, which was adopted.

After half an hour the process continued.
Prosecutor Smoljanović asked to speak.
"Comrade Chairman, comrade jurors, by observing the defendant's behavior in the courtroom, I have reached a conclusion that his contempt of this court should not go unsanctioned. He should be punished as an example to others so that they wouldn't do the same. I believe that a small punishment wouldn't be effective, so I ask the court to carefully consider the defendant's situation. That would be all for the time being."

"Comrade jurors, comrade Chairman, I ask to speak," said the appointed defense attorney, Lieutenant-Colonel Grujo Čurgus.

"By all means, comrade lieutenant-colonel, the floor is yours."

"I believe that my client has been wrongly accused. The court has failed to prove that he committed the criminal offense as described in Article 105, Subsections 1 and 2. He has restrained from reacting much more than would normally be expected. I ask comrade prosecutor to put himself in the defendant's position; how would you feel if somebody forced a confession out of you?"

Chairman of the court, Lieutenant-Colonel Kapetanovic, raised his hand and said: "Comrade Lieutenant-Colonel, do you have a degree in law?"

"Yes, comrade, I do."

"And this is the way you defend your client? I am warning you, if you keep this up, you might find yourself sitting right next to him!"

The defense attorney asked for a five-minute break and the guard was ordered to take me to the waiting room.

Fifteen minutes later the interrogation continued.

"Defendant, are you aware of the fact that your behavior and honesty before this court can affect the length of your punishment?"

"Yes, I am, but this can hardly be called punishment, because punishment is what happens to you if you commit a criminal offense of some sort. Only then can somebody be punished. But this? I cannot call this punishment. This is pure enslavement and not punishment."

"I am warning you, watch your mouth! Comrades, we're running out of time for today. This process will continue at another time."

The process did continue, but without me in the courtroom, even though I was in the building. Realizing I could have a nervous breakdown, the court decided not to call me at all; instead, I was presented with the court's final decision, which said: *In the name of the people, the accused Josip Zoretić is sentenced to seven years in a maximum-security prison.*

The day was December 28, 1962.

*Goli Otok*

# Purgatory

I refused to sign the verdict and asked to appeal to the Supreme Military Court in Belgrade. The defense representative informed me that he would appeal, but at that time there was no way for me to really know that he would or if he even did. While waiting for Belgrade's response, I was put in a room with two men who were, like me, convicted and sentenced, but to five years in prison instead of seven. They were both Croats from Lika and they both ended up there the same way I did.

We were later joined by Rihard, a Slovene from the town of Hoče near Maribor and later by a Serb named Ćiro. Ćiro was sent by the investigator to listen to and report our private conversations. The mole introduced himself to us as a Slovene, but he could hardly have passed as one. He spoke some Slovenian, but not enough for us to believe him. He had been commander of a watchtower in Slovenia so he had picked up some things. He would always rant and complain about the government, just to try and get us to say something. Once he squealed on Rihard for insulting the Belgrade government and the Serbs, which landed Rihard into solitary and he was badly beaten.

On his return to our holding cell a fight between the two of them broke out and Ćiro was transferred to another room. Rihard underwent one more torturing session in the basement of the building. He came back with four of his teeth missing.

"What have they done to you, Rihard?"

"Well, it could have been worse."

Suddenly the door swung open.

"What are you two talking about?!" asked the squad leader of the military police.

"Out of the room, grab a brush, some soap and a mop and make this hallway glitter!"

It was not that difficult to work because I had no fresh bruises or swellings, but Rihard barely got through two hours of scrubbing the concrete floor with a heavy brush. Even his head was all swollen. And he didn't get any sleep later that night.

Similar scenes happened every single day and every single night. Victims were picked randomly and not everyone was dealt with in the same way.

Unfortunately, I too contributed to the sleeplessness of my inmates. As soon as I'd fall asleep I'd start screaming during violent nightmares. The pills the doctor gave me weren't helping so the police would come by at night to help keep me awake. They would shake me just as I would fall asleep.

This continued for over two months, until March 13, when I was transferred to a transport room on the first floor, unaware of where I was heading and without word of the status of my appeal. Several prisoners from the Zagreb military prison were already there, as well as a number of men from the Sarajevo military prison. We were all waiting for a transport which arrived from Belgrade some time before the break of dawn.

Half an hour later we were all handcuffed, two by two, but two men from the same prison were never handcuffed together. We were put on a bus with curtains covering the windows, followed by eight officers and NCOs armed with machine guns and hand grenades.

The bus, along with three police cars, headed

for the city of Rijeka then turned south along the coast. We headed toward the town of Jurjevo near Senj, where a boat called "Cer" was waiting for us.

Members of the militia, wearing blue uniforms, were watching us closely. One officer carrying a heavy machine gun was standing on the command bridge. Other men in uniforms encircled us.

A mariner lowered a plank from the ship and a voice was heard giving us orders: "One pair behind the other, just like you are tied to each other! I want to see you on board immediately, is that clear, you scum?!"

A silence fell – you could have heard a pin drop. We were now aware that we were headed for Goli Otok – a lawless island about which not much was known; only that it was hell in the Adriatic.

*Josip Zoretić*

# Hell's Gate

*The belief in a supernatural source of evil is not necessary; men alone are quite capable of every wickedness.*
                                        Joseph Conrad


Cer pushed off from the shore. A fat officer came among us. I later learned his name was Nikola Radaković, called Radak.

"Is there anyone among you who knows where we are headed to?" he asked.

Nobody spoke a word.

"So you have no idea, have you? Not even one person knows we're going to Goli Otok?!"

Stevo from Rijeka said he knew.

"And how do you know this? Maybe you've been on the island before?"

"No sir, I'm from Rijeka and I often went fishing near here with my father so that's how I know," answered Stevo.

"Nobody else? Why don't I run a check?"

Ten minutes later he returned and asked which one of us was from the town of Gračac.

"I am," said a man.

"It's you, is it? And yet you kept quiet, you son of a bitch! You know well what's in store for you. You ran away before but here you are again..."

He wasn't actually a runaway, but a repeat offender.

The ship was sailing toward Goli Otok and one could already see stone dust bursting out of a chimney in a stone-grinding plant.

The returnee whispered and explained to us what was what, but Radak noticed, called him and shut him in a small luggage compartment.

## Goli Otok

When the boat landed ashore we were received by Ranković's men who were delighted to see us. We left the boat two by two and went straight to the admissions section. I never saw the man from Gračac again.

In the admissions section, called the Quarantine, prison guards welcomed us with the words: "Well, well, would you look at that! A hundred and something of them, and, look here, they've all committed almost the same criminal offense. Now get into that room and put all your belongings into one pile and take off all of your clothes. As soon as you're naked line up one behind the other!"

There were two barbers that shaved us. The older one was responsible for the head and armpits; the younger one responsible for the area around our genitals. The younger one nervously told us: "Do take hold of that misery of yours! Can't you see how many of you I still have to shave?"

When twelve men were finished they'd be lined up and sent to the bathroom.

"There are twelve of us with commander Jovo," said someone.

"Get going then! Here's the soap."

"And how do we make water run?" asked a man from Zagorje.

"Stand under one of the showers and wait for the order. Don't make a move unless you're given the order."

Finally water started running, but it was cold. Oh, how cold it was!

"Hah-hah, you aren't at your mother's or in a hotel to expect hot water! Soap yourselves faster! . . . Stop, leave the soap on the floor!"

Again the water started running, but just for a very short time. I didn't even have time to rinse the lather between my legs.

We received prison uniforms, made of quite good fabric but so badly sewn that it was impossible to make them fit properly. The spring/summer uniforms were light green and made of a slightly lighter material than the brown winter uniforms made of the material used for making sacks. The murderers and other criminals got ones that were better quality and in better condition than the political prisoners. I received one that was used and worn out. They didn't give us any shoes but some sort of galoshes with rubber soles and two strap buckles made especially for the rocky land on Goli Otok.

The inauguration ended and night came. It was bedtime, but there was no room in the beds for all of us. The beds were iron with strawmattresses – stuffed with hay in potato-sack-like material. At least they were clean. Later on we were required to stuff our mattress when the hay was changed in them, but this time it was done for us. You couldn't really get any rest because five people had to squeeze into one double bed. It was more exhausting than resting.

We got up at 4:15 a.m. Banging was heard everywhere along with yells to get up. They didn't really have to yell all that much – everyone was scared and got up quickly.

All those who had slept on the sides of the beds were to make the beds and the rest of us had to go and do exercises – morning calisthenics while it was still pitch dark. The lineup was so long that some men standing at the end of the line were in complete darkness because the light from the stairway couldn't reach them.

Cold Bura was blowing from the Velebit Mountain at speeds of about 80 km/h, which was usual for this part of the country. It brought dust from the sea surface – sea mist and saltwater that one feels on the lips. It also made our faces turn white and caused lichens.

"Enough with the exercises," said one of the officers, who we referred to as "Blue Angels" because of their blue uniforms. The Blue Angels were mostly Serbs from Croatia whose parents collaborated with the Partisans during WWII, so their hatred toward the Croats, Bosnians, and Albanians was enormous. To make things even sadder, these policemen were almost illiterate. They spoke some local dialect of their own, Lika or Kordun variety, instead of the standard that they were supposed to use.

"Listen now, you'll be able to wash yourselves the way you want, with no procedural orders. You'll have three minutes so hurry up. If you don't finish, you won't have time to do it later!"

Lining up for breakfast was next – black coffee with no sugar but with some marmalade floating on it, and, of course, bread which was the same as on the outside.

After breakfast there was another lineup outside and a work schedule was made. Some prisoners were sent to build roads while others, including myself, collected stones by hand and carried them, also by hand, to a pile, which lasted for hours until 2 p.m.

Again we formed a double file to return.

"Come forward and fill the line densely," ordered commander Jovo.

"The one who was talking about how far the mainland and other islands are will now step forward! Is that person here?!"

Nobody came forward.

"Is he here or not? You just won't step forward, will you? Rahelić, step forward now!"

Rahelić stepped forward.

"Take him straight to solitary," ordered Jovo to his assistant.

"Fill the line densely!" said Jovo's voice again.

"Now go to lunch in a single file. Take off your hats in front of the dining room!"

Another Blue Angel was standing in the dining room saying: "Take the first available seat and don't leave any empty. Don't start eating without the order! . . . Start now, but not a word!"

Sauerkraut, pretty badly prepared, was eaten in a matter of seconds.

"Enough! Stand up and leave the room one by one!"

The same plates were refilled quickly.

"Another group of thirty, step in one by one!"

The rest of the men were standing in the line and waiting for their turn to eat. Even though they were starving, they would rather have had no lunch at all than stand in the line for so long since they were all so exhausted, barely able to stand.

"And now, move it!" came the order. But Jovo interrupted. "No. They have to learn the House Rules. You can see they don't know what's proper. We should get them acquainted with the way of life here, in the Quarantine and later in the Wires. Now, everyone, get going to the ping-pong hall and start learning the House Rules!"

*Goli Otok*

# House Rules

*We may brave human laws, but we cannot resist natural ones.*
                             Jules Verne


The House Rules were based neither on law nor order and didn't even remotely relate to a proper human existence. Everything was defined by labor – not a word about health care or about life suitable for a human being living in a civilized age. Everything was forbidden except for labor, twenty-four hour labor when necessary, without a break of any kind.

"And at the end", said Jovo, "the signature. Read it slowly and repeat it out loud so that by tomorrow morning every single one of you knows the full name of the warden of the correctional facility!"

On the bottom was the butcher's symbolic signature:

Correctional facility board
Correctional facility warden
Goli Otok, Rab
Rade Radović

"So now you know you must take off your hat and stand up straight when somebody passes near you, be it the warden, a police officer, a clerk, or civilians who will be your commanding chiefs at work after six weeks in the admissions section. Failure to take off your hat will be punished with scrubbing. You can only do the scrubbing while others are asleep, and it takes two hours. The scrubbing is done with sea water, and should anyone get caught scrubbing with fresh, drinking water, he will be punished with five scrubbings, which means one full night plus two more hours. You cannot have help with scrubbing; you have to work it off yourselves. All of these punishments are given to those who haven't learned to show respect to their elders and who try to have things their way. But here you have to comply! It's awkward for the thugs but they all give way in the end and see it's for the better. These are not threats! I'm just speaking from experience!"

A "clerk" was what they called the persons in charge of altering our opinions, because apparently we weren't learned enough to be able to understand the modern socialism that they were building. They never used torture. They would continuously attempt to brainwash us, attempting to get us to admit our "mistakes" and routinely telling is that we should listen to them because they knew better.

The civilians were managers of the plants that produced goods and were employees of the *Velebit Rijeka Industrial Conglomerate*, the company whose name the goods made by prisoner labor were sold under. They were not employees of the prison.

On that same evening there were thirty of us doing the scrubbing because we forgot to take off our hats. We weren't scrubbing rooms but the stone stairs, each stair twenty times, one after the other.

The next day was another day with the exact same amount of work, which was unbearable. We were exhausted. Our arms and legs hurt and we couldn't fill the quota so we were beaten. Many men collapsed, especially the ones that were put in solitary for minor mistakes, like the one Rahelić made when he told us the distance between the islands of Rab and Goli.

That incident indicated that there were some among us who were collaborating with the prison police, because when Rahelić was talking about the distance between the islands, no prison police were near enough to hear what was said. This sort of information was not to be known or discussed because someone might use it to plan an escape. It was this piece of information that brought Rahelić ten nights in solitary and ten days of hard labor under the strict supervision of a Blue Angel.

"What are those men over there doing, the ones walking in a file? I wonder where they're going," I asked.

"Shush! They're 102!"

"How many? 102? How do you know the exact number?"

"No, that's what they're called. It's the disciplinary section of the island."

"And how did they end up there?"

"I've heard they're mostly haranguers there."

"What are haranguers?"

"They're the ones that don't obey the House Rules. They disobey and that's not allowed, so they have to do the most difficult work around here. And they're watched closely at all times."

"And what happens if they still disobey?"

"Then they're up for straightening. And if you don't fill your quota, again straightening."

"Straightening," or *peglanje,* was the term used for torture.

"That's . . . that's impossible to bear!"

"There are some that don't make it through."

"What do you mean they don't make it through, they've got to!"

"Oh no pal, take a look behind the Quarantine, there's a graveyard there . . . and over there by the power station another graveyard. Both full of men that couldn't take it . . . the so-called softies. They're even called the softies' graveyards."

"And what if a relative or someone wants to know about them?"

"They just say the man is missing, that he's run away."

"How do you know all this? You came on the same boat as I did!"

"Some older convicts told me all about it."

I later found all this to be true when I accidentally ended up among the graves while searching for soil. I saw piles of stone and on top of each pile was one larger stone with numbers carved into it. Upon arrival at the correctional facility every inmate was registered and one's registration number was also one's identity number. The numbers on the graves were their personal identity numbers. That was all the information that existed about the men who lay under those stones.

But registration numbers were not always unique. During my time on Goli Otok, registration numbers were repeated three times – purposeful false record-keeping in order to hide the true extent of how many suffered on Goli Otok.

*Goli Otok*

## Wires and Sections

After six weeks in the Admissions section everybody was transferred to the "Wires." That was the name of the colony in which a large number of middle-class convicts, in terms of causing trouble on the island, lived, including political prisoners.

"Wires" was a suitable name for it – a strong electrified wire fence with four-meter-high concrete pillars surrounding it, erected by Cominform supporters in 1948. It was watched at all times by the Blue Angels from their watchtowers, also made of concrete, armed with machine guns, radios and trained dogs which routinely kept us awake at night with their barking.

To make things even worse, sleeping arrangements were such that men from three different shifts slept in the same room – they'd disturb each other going to and coming back from work.

The first shift would get up at 4:20, both in the winter and the summer, and would work from 6:00 a.m. to 2:15 p.m. The second shift would work from 2:30 p.m. to 10:30 p.m. with a fifteen-minute break called "tea." The third shift was in charge of cleaning the machines and repairing any malfunctions that occurred during the previous shifts, without a break.

A siren announced it was time to wake up and it was stronger than that of a fire engine. Its sound sometimes seemed to tear my heart apart, especially when I was asleep.

Every day we woke up obliged to play different scenarios under the direction of Ranković's men.

Not all convicts were treated the same way

on Goli Otok; the Serbs were mostly treated well because almost all of the officers were Serbs. Almost all of them were uneducated Croatian Orthodox Serbs from the region of Lika, claiming to be pure Serbs – the mortal enemies of Croats, Slovenes and Albanians. They hated the Croats the most and had an excuse for it: they said that during the era of Ante Pavelić the Croats slaughtered an immense number of innocent Serbs in Croatia. Their payback included seeking revenge against the children, including those who weren't even born at the time, of those who fought against them.

The police officers and the management decided whom they would spare. The only exceptions were the officers who didn't perform their duties well outside the island – they were punished by being sent to work on Goli Otok. Such officers generally didn't want to torture the convicts and were further punished with up to 50 percent off their salaries for not doing so.

Convicts' self-management was established and only the worst criminals, men without feelings, could be appointed the secretary. The position of secretary was more for public consumption, to make it appear that the convicts had a representative. There was no shortage of hardcore criminals willing to take on the role, since it was well-known that your sentence could be reduced if you proved useful enough to the correctional facility. It meant a great deal to have your sentence reduced from twenty to fifteen years and they would do anything to have it lowered.

The man appointed secretary in 1964 was a man who, not wanting to marry his girlfriend, forced his unborn baby out of her womb with his own feet by jumping on her stomach when she was eight months pregnant. He was convicted and sentenced to fifteen years in prison for his crime. When he arrived to the island to serve his sentence the prison management realized he was right for the job and he was allowed to fill the post, which he willingly accepted with open arms. The police would severely punish anyone who disobeyed his orders, but he never gave orders to anyone directly.

Groups of men worked in various sections, such as the stone processing plant, called the "Concreting." In that section only those registered as unreformable worked, which included most of the political prisoners. The prisoners in this section were always careful not to make any mistake when working, which wasn't really possible. When somebody did something not to the liking of the police the police would react severely, mostly by kicking or beating them with a billy club on the spot. Whenever there was a government official around, anyone else besides prisoners, we had to refer to the billy club as "the educational baton."

There was also a metal processing plant called the "Locksmiths' Section," and a section called the "Correctional" section for preparing food, washing clothes and blankets, and shoe preparation and cleaning.

All of these groups were run by prisoners known as "Room Seniors." They didn't have much to do. Their only duty was to find out who was saying what, if anyone was planning to escape, how others did their jobs, and who was hanging out with whom. Naturally, they had their informants, or snitchers, who used various methods to try to find out what was necessary. They sent the information on through the Room Seniors to the Secretary, who then sent it on to prison management.

If someone was accused of something, little investigation was conducted to establish the truth of the matter. They would just send you to 102, also known as section C, or officially as the disciplinary section.

The Room Senior was authorized to send a man to 102 without notifying the prison management. Such laws made every single moment, not to mention every day, every year, unbearable, especially for those of us who still had our self-respect and wouldn't talk to suspicious guys about anything and everything.

In order to achieve the goal of punishment, the island enforced Hitler's slogan: "Don't allow the prisoners enough time to think," so we had no free time from dusk till dawn. We were always either lining up for something or laboring.

After breakfast the Room Senior would lead the file to the fence from where the guards would lead it to work and supervise them until the return to the Wires.

The file had to be lined up better than in the military – four-man files that were several hundred meters long. Little did they know about pedagogy, they sorted everything out by beating us. Any minor mistake in the lineup, for example if your hat was crooked, if you weren't lined up properly with the others, or if you said something, resulted in a beating with a club. A lit cigarette would bring you a straightening session in 102 followed by time in solitary, and this was performed at will by the officers that were present. If they heard someone say something without seeing who said it, they would stop the file to find out. If no one came forward that entire part of the file would be beaten as if they all had spoken.

There were some officers who didn't take pleasure in beating us up, but they had to do it because they had orders to do so. But, Pemper, two Grahovacs (father and son), Marković, Miloš Novković, who we called "Mrki" (brown bear) because of his dark complexion, Dimitrijević, Pičuljan called "Cokula," Malić, and Jovo Korica in the Wires enjoyed torturing the prisoners.

The special squad used to perform torturing sessions in 102 in an insulated building, so they indulged as much as they liked. "Little" Jovica, about a meter and a half tall, or about 5 feet, could hit harder than Salatović who was about two meters in height, or 6 feet 7 inches. Lazo, two meters in height, Radaković (called Radak), 110 kilograms and bony, and many others all mastered their bashing techniques under the tutorship of Colonel Nikolić and the Militia's Lieutenant-Colonel Stojko Jakovljevica.

A file started moving from the fence toward the plants and it looked as if it were unending. Several times someone was heard begging, "Please don't, commander, I haven't done anything!"

"Son of a cow . . . Do you think I'm deaf and blind?!"

Some men would sob by the end of the trip toward the plants due to the beatings, and some couldn't even catch their breath at times, which was the case with me several times.

Those walking in front of the victim sometimes couldn't help taking a look back at what was happening even though it meant running the risk of getting beaten.

In case of rain, and the island only has heavy showers, the police wouldn't allow for the walking ceremony to be postponed or rushed; the file had to be as punctual as clockwork. The officers dressed depending on the weather. When they came into the working halls, the UDBA (State Security Administration members – Yugoslavia's secret police), in civilian clothes, called the Bosses, would be waiting to tell us who would do what. Those of us that they considered stupid would get easier jobs. For anyone who seemed a bit more able, they would get more difficult jobs in order to break them down mentally.

"Here, Mirko, these are the new power-holders," said Radaković, who led the file into the hall for stone processing to his superior, Mirko Čor, an UDBA member.
"Hah hah hah, they're smart, aren't they? But we're even smarter than them; we've beaten them to it. They're patriots, you see, they've come to work for free! But we'll pay them for it."
"Okay fellows, how many are you?" Čor was rubbing his hands. "You tall guy, how many of them have you brought?"
"You piece of shit, is this what we've taught you? Not taking your hat off while talking to the Boss? And what about you?" he said, pointing at another worker.
"Boss, I'm convict Anđelo Lazar, personal identity number 103, five and a half years."
"See him? Hat off, standing still and not like a sissy! What about you?"
"Thirteen years."
"That means you're a good worker. You've done well and I hope you work well here, right? It

shouldn't be too hard, he's smart and probably aware of the kind of place he's in. If he gets any weird ideas we'll make sure he loses them. And you?"

"Me Boss I Priština Albania, Bocoku Salih."

"Well, what do you know, he can't even speak properly and he wants to run the business here! Enough with the commentary. Now, group according to the number of years to serve, I'm sure you all know who's got how much time to do. Okay, you to the Separation, the ones up to here to the press, and the rest to the grinders, is that clear? Get to work now! And don't anyone leave work without letting me know! You have to report to me even if you have to go to the latrine. Whoever disobeys should not be surprised at the consequences! You may go now!"

The Separation was the factory plant where large amounts of different colored stone were ground to make tones of terrazzo tiles every day, which produced enormous amounts of stone dust.

The tiles were mostly shipped to Libya and other Arab countries to be used in mosques. We could tell where the tiles were shipped because the shipping labels were written in English as well as Arabic. They left the island with the label *Velebit Rijeka Industrial Conglomerate*. It was rumored that some of the stone used at the United Nations building in New York was actually cut on Goli Otok.

Work was conducted under severe conditions – with strong winds in the winter, terrible heat in the summer, and always under the strict supervision of Blue Angels. Within ten minutes the thick clouds of stone dust covered everything except for the eyes and teeth, if you still had any left, which you could see through sticky lips. In order to grind two hundred tons of stone within the required time, which was for as long as the machinery could stand, four men had to be lowered into the throttle of the mill, which may seem impossible to endure if you considered the breakfast we received: black coffee with a bit of marmalade floating on it and some quite good bread. But practice has shown that hatred can help a man endure anything.

Long-term labor in the Separation caused tuberculosis and silicosis, but the plant management was kind enough not to let the sick anti-state items die in the Separation; not because they were humane but because of the risk of low productivity in the plant. Whenever someone became ill, new workers, new anti-state items came to fill the post, while the sick received no treatment but were instead sent to work in a cleaner air environment. If someone died he'd be covered with stones in the graveyard, with his identity number carved into the gravestone, the same identity number he received upon arrival at the island.

"Hey, Ivan, have you heard that last night two men from Zagreb ran away from the woodwork plant?"

I never worked in the woodwork plant.

"I've heard about it, but it seems they're still looking for them. You see, Vila Velebit and the speedboats keep patrolling the waters and the officers and dogs are searching the island. If they made it to sea without being noticed then they stand a chance, but if they're still on the island they're finished! It's a wonder that no one snitched on them. We'll hear about it in time."

Vila Velebit was a smaller and slower boat used to patrol around the island, and was never used to transport prisoners.

"I don't believe anyone knew about it. You know you can have your sentence reduced if you tell them things like that. The murderers would definitely have taken advantage of the information. But they're in trouble if they don't make it, they'll never see the light of day again. What's the time? I haven't heard if the mill siren marked the break."

"I haven't heard it either. Are we near filling the quota?"

"Four wagons more."

"I guess it hasn't whistled yet."

"Hurry up, twenty more minutes! If you don't finish you'll have to stay here till six and that means no lunch for you," yelled the foreman, who worked under the Room Senior, a member of the convicts' self-management.

"How much longer?" I asked.

"Five more minutes, one wagon, thank God!"

"Do you believe in God?"

"Yeah, and you?"

"Not anymore I don't. I used to. If there was a God, he wouldn't allow for this to happen."

"Are you through up there?" asked the men who were taking the materials to the Separation.

"Yeah, finished!"

"Oh, Janez, and you Ivo! I wouldn't recognize you if it weren't for your voices!"

"Well what did you expect? You don't look any better, all covered with dust. Where's the brigadier?"

"He left with the commandant. They wouldn't be caught dead breathing in the dust."

"Hurry up, the siren's wailed already! We don't want to be late for the lineup!"

"Stand in a file of four, bastards! Ante, are they all here?"

"How many did we have this morning?"

"Five hundred and sixty seven."

"Two are missing. They didn't line up nicely. Approach four by four!"

"Two are missing indeed. No, they're in section C, punished for disobeying the brigadier."

"Are they those new guys?"

"No. One of them is that priest from Slavonia and the other's a Montenegrin. Move it, bastards!"

Only about the first five hundred meters of the road was paved, the rest was only planned and still waiting to be finished but we were still required to march in a straight line.

The fence at the entrance into the Wires was where the transfer of command took place. We then went to the dining room and had to stand in a single file and wait for food under the supervision of a Blue Angel and a Room Senior.

"Hurry up with the lunch! Get going! You'll stay in the Wires today! There are stones to be restacked in the Wires!"

"Would you look at this, Dušan! For two days these stones have been sent here from the people working in the woodwork plant and today we're sending them back."

The convicts were given so much work to do that one couldn't rest for a moment. All this went on so as not to allow us time to think. But this tactic had bad repercussions on efficiency, especially with the second-shift workers.

No one was allowed to leave their post; we had to inform the officer on duty even if we went to the latrine.

"Slowly, it's a long time until seven o'clock."

"At least they'll leave us alone then."

"What are you two smartasses doing loitering like that? Move it," said a poltroon, "or else you'll be talking to the Room Senior!"

"We're tired, we can't go any faster."

"Tired, are you? Well, the others are just as tired, and see, they're much quicker carrying the stones. Alright, this is just a warning; we'll see how well you do tomorrow."

"Stop working, it's seven o'clock! Stand in a file of four! Right, now straight to the dining room!"

After giving us slops to eat we again had to line up to go and polish shoes and finally had some time off from 7:30 to 8 p.m.

At the sound of the siren we were supposed to stand in a file of five while three men did the counting of everyone in the Wires. If the number was wrong we would all have to stand outside waiting until the police found the ones that were missing. It didn't matter if it was raining, the procedure was always the same, and there was no place to get warm, no heating of course, except for in the management building, and ordinary convicts weren't allowed there. If you got through a day without getting beaten, if you never violated the rules, that day would be a success.

"You, number one forty-six . . ."

"You don't know my name?"

"Josip, isn't it?"

"No. Yes, it is, just kidding."

"The guys from the woodwork plant drowned, you know."

"How do you know?"

"That's what I've heard."

"Maybe it's for the better. They could have been caught alive!"

*Goli Otok*

# Failed Attempt

The next day was no different from any other, witnessing a torture or two, and then at 2:00 the order came that we were all to line up quickly along with the other shift that was supposed to start working. Once we were all lined up a lieutenant ordered us to march straight to the wharf where Blue Angels took over the command and lined us up around so that we could all see the wharf.

Two corpses, aged around twenty, were taken out of a speedboat. The lieutenant ordered one brigadier to take off their clothes. The bodies were full of knife wounds, both on the front and back.

"Listen now," said the lieutenant. "See these two? They grew up together, went to school together and attempted to escape together. They made a timber raft and took with them knives to fight off the sharks or anyone on the mainland. When they got to the middle of the Senj Channel the raft started sinking and even though they were inseparable friends they each tried to save themselves. They pulled their knives on each other and as you can see they stabbed each other to death. See how precious life is?"

There were sighs among the convicts.

"If the raft floats well in the shallow water it is even safer in the deep. What they're saying can't be true, they must have killed them, just as they've already killed many others."

"Who's talking?!"

As they couldn't tell who it was right away they kept asking and a man came forward.

"I'm the one, convict number one forty-eight. That's the truth," said the man from Split who came to the island two months before graduation from the Naval Academy.

The consequences were severe. It would have been better not to have made the comment, but the lies that the lieutenant were saying couldn't have gone unopposed, no matter what the consequences.

*Goli Otok*

# Fight

There was a large number of Bosnians and Albanians on Goli Otok. The Albanians thought that those who couldn't speak their language were their enemies and couldn't be trusted, which was what they had learned under Ranković's terror.

Bečir was their leader and was imprisoned for war issues and sentenced to death, but since he had been captured long after the war was over his sentence was reduced to twenty years in prison. He was sort of a lawgiver who instructed the Albanians on what to do to protect their country from disaster.

The reaction of the Albanians to any injustice they suffered was plain physical force, but only if it was against other convicts; they weren't brave enough when it came to dealing with the Blue Angels. Fights were not uncommon and most of them were against Bosnians. Hearing someone swear was enough and the retribution took place later on, usually at night.

The Albanians shrank from no means when attacking a victim and neither did the Bosnians, but only if the fight involved these two nationalities. Men of other nationalities avoided Albanians because of their behavior, and Bosnians acted the same toward everybody, especially because their religion was mainly different from that of the others.

On one particular occasion in the stone processing plant, Mirko Čor assigned one shovel per press when two were needed. He demanded that the quota be filled, which led to fights breaking out between Bosnians and Albanians for the other shovel.

"Let go of the shovel!"

"I need it!"

"Give it to me you motherfucker! Stupid Šok!"

Šok was the nickname we used to refer to Albanians from Kosovo.

"You fucking Bosnian, I'll get you . . . . "

A blow to the chin followed.

The commandant heard something was going on and went to see what it was.

"What's going on, Šok?" he asked. When the reply was "nothing, comrade," he left.

"I'll show you tonight when you're asleep."

"Shut up, *stupid Šok!*, I'll crush you like a little baby. We'll continue this tonight in the Wires, seven-thirty to eight."

But the Albanians didn't wait until the evening. The fight started the moment they returned from work, in the dining room during lunch, and spread throughout the Wires. Three hundred Albanians on one side and three hundred Bosnians on the other. They used stones, knives, planks and anything they could get their hands on. There weren't enough Blue Angels to stop the fight so by the time their backup with dogs arrived the fight had escalated. There were moments when they would hit someone from their own side.

After the fight the damage was obvious: fractured heads, ears cut off, broken arms and legs, stab wounds . . . and eventually new trials off the island and transfers to section C.

Croats and Serbs also hated each other but there were no large fights between them, even though insults were said on every possible occasion.

*Goli Otok*

"Hey, Slobodan, did you take a blow or two in this fight?" I asked.

"No, I didn't. I'm from Bosnia but I won't have any part of this. My eight years are more than enough. Those who are crazy enough to fight are free to do so, but I don't want to be afraid of Albanians at night. I'm just wondering who keeps sending them here to the island. Don't they have a prison for them down there?"

"Sure they don't! Ranković knows well what he's doing."

"What do you mean *Ranković*? You Croats hate the Serbs so you blame it all on Ranković just because he's Serbian."

"Well he filled all the prisons with Croats, of course I don't like him!"

"You're still dreaming of an independent Croatia, are you? Well, it's only a dream, I'm telling you! Serbs keep helping you and you still hate them."

"Yeah right! Serbs are doing just the opposite. All the income from tourism on the Adriatic and all the foreign money goes to the Bank of Belgrade to pay off the debt of the entire country and Croatia gets nothing out of it. Since the war till today we've been giving everything to Belgrade and never got anything back."

"You seem troubled by that. Ask the Germans for help. You fought on their side, have them give you what you want!"

"What a loser! If you're such a patriot why did they send you here then? You ignorant fool! You barbarians lived in caves until a while ago and now you're enslaving other nations and you're still too stupid to see your dear Ranković defeated by other nations!"

"What are you, an idiot? Have you forgotten

I'm *Serbian* from Bosnia? Thank God we're here; if we were on the outside I'd show you what it means to have Serbian blood running through the veins . . . "

"Ooh, now you're scaring me! My Room Senior's coming, I don't want any trouble with him."

"Waiting for something, Slobodan? To the lineup and get to work!" said the Room Senior.

"Right away," he replied.

"Where have you been all this time?"

"I was watching that fight."

"The fight's finished long ago. Both of you, line up and go straight behind the Quarantine to gather soil, each with his own brigadier. If you've had lunch already, fine; if not, no more lunch today, that is an order."

"Comrade brigadier, why do we have to look for soil when there's none on the island?" I asked.

"Shut it! Don't you ask any questions! Giving orders is not your job; you are here only to obey and not to ask, understood?"

"Yes, comrade brigadier!"

Over a hundred of us couldn't find a lump of soil from 3 p.m. until 6:40, but we had to be in the Wires on time. We finished eating our dinner but the night that followed, and every night, wasn't pleasant because the so-called control lights, by which we were controlled during the night, were on all the time.

Not far away from me slept a Greek priest named Andoni Stavro. I asked him: "Listen Stavro, you've been sleeping under these lights for over ten years, shouldn't you be accustomed to them by now?"

"If you stay here long enough, you'll have a hard time getting used to them as well, my son," he said.

"Why do they keep the lights on? I mean, there are lights outside and they keep watching us anyway."

"It's because of the homosexuals. There are men here that like that sort of thing and they can be punished for it. They can't do anything during the day, and the lights are here so that they wouldn't do anything in bed."

"I don't see how anyone would even think about it after working."

"There are those that don't get difficult jobs."

"Who the fuck is talking?! If you can't sleep then go out!"

Stavro really wasn't in a mood for sleeping. He had several healed fractured bones and whenever the weather was changing he felt a strong pain in them. He would often joke about it, saying Goli Otok had given him a free weather station.

*Josip Zoretić*

# Officer-in-Charge

The morning came and the endless line of men was headed for another new day full of torment.

"Marijan, who's that fat and tall civilian? You've been here a while now, I suppose you should know him," I asked one of my fellow prisoners.

"Why do you ask?"

"I've seen him around. He's been watching all the workplaces and he never said a word to anyone."

"Don't even ask, you'll meet him soon enough. He's a Partisan colonel; he's now with the police, also as a colonel, but a civilian. He works as a convict reeducator and from time to time he replaces the warden when he's away. He's going to be your Officer-in-Charge [*referent*] because you're in Number 2. He and two assistants are in charge of Number 2. Isn't he well-nourished! War pension, regular salary, bonus for living away from society, bonus for dangerous circumstances. No wonder he's so huge."

"Are they armed?"

"Not anymore. They used to be, but sometimes the convicts took their guns and started shooting people. Members of the Cominform did that more often than others, but they'd end up dead as well. Don't tell anyone you heard it from me."

"No problem."

A Room Senior addressed us all by the entrance to the Wires: "Everybody get to work except the six men I'll call out now. They are going to meet the Officer-in-Charge. Hope you're all here! . . . Look at him, ripped trousers! You can't see the Officer-in-Charge looking like that" he said, referring to me. I was one of the six.

"Dušan, take your trousers off and give them to him till he comes back. His trousers will be mended during the night."

The Room Senior told the clerk to let us into the building to see the Officer-in-Charge. We entered a large lobby with three benches where we sat waiting to be called in. Prison staff kept passing us by and we had to stand up and stand still until they passed.

I was the first one to be called; "Send number one forty-six in."

The Room Senior took me to room 11. I was not allowed to touch the doorknobs – an officer opened and closed the door behind me. I introduced myself: "Comrade Officer-in-Charge, convict Zoretić Josip, registration number one forty-six, reporting as ordered."

"Look at you, you used to be a soldier, is that the right posture? I'm warning you to answer my questions truthfully and honestly. I've seen you work and you're not good at all. Why? Bad workers are sent to the disciplinary section and when they become good workers they are sent back to the Wires. What is the reason you haven't been working well?"

"I was seriously tortured during the investigation and at the moment I can't perform better."

"Right, you admitted to nothing, you were convicted on the grounds of suspicion. Well, we're not going to beg you to do it here. I'm giving you three months to think about everything and when you're ready, inform your Room Senior that you are willing to talk to me. But only if you plan to be honest with me, so we can set everything straight. I'll write down the date when you are to appear here again, and don't make me send for you first or I'll have you sent to the C section. Also, you have quite some time to do here and you'd be better off on our side than on the side of the convicts. You could tell us about what other convicts are saying."

"I couldn't do that, comrade. I've never sunk so low in my life and I don't intend to do so here on the island. I'd rather die."

"Fine, you don't have to do anything you don't want to, but think about it. Three months will pass quickly. You see, people who realize their mistakes and repent are treated differently here. Those that are stubborn get special treatment. Since you're cheeky and short-tempered I'm forbidding you any correspondence for the next six months. That's six letters altogether. If the maximum security measures don't work for you I'll change it to something that does work. Now, tell me, who have you been spending time with in the Wires?"

"No one, comrade, I don't even have time to wipe my nose, and I don't associate with anyone."

"Liar! You and that Novak from Maribor have been talking every night before the evening recount. What have you been talking about?"

"That is not true. He always keeps quiet and I have nothing to say to him."

"I know everything. Would you like me to tell you what the two of you talk about? On the first night you talked about the investigation and about your relatives. The second night you talked about his relatives in Sweden and the third night about life on the island. What, your knees are starting to shake? That's it then, Novak is going to the disciplinary section tonight. And because you weren't honest you'll do five scrubbings. The Room Senior will tell you all about how it is done."

The Room Senior was listening to our conversation so he explained it to me right away: "A scrubbing lasts two hours. It's done only at night. Only the stairs are scrubbed, not the rooms."

The Officer-in-Charge continued the interrogation: "You have some relatives abroad, don't you?"

"I do," I answered.

"We have it all written down here. They got away but you fell into our hands. Your father supported the Ustaše and went down. If you act like him you're going down as well. Who do you think we are? We beat six of Hitler's elite divisions in a matter of days, and you handful of nobodies think you can take us. It's because of the social outcasts like you that we have to spend money on reeducation when it could be spent on something more necessary. But never mind, what we want is to make a man see his own mistakes. We want him to repent and become a truly useful member of our society. That's all, you can go now."

"Thank you, Comrade Officer-in-Charge."

Back in the lobby Lazo asked me how it went. "Great," I said. "I got five scrubbings and no correspondence for six months, all because of my bad performance at work, and I haven't even been beaten once for it. He's generous so he's handing out punishments. You're up next; I saw your file next to mine on the desk."

Lazo was then called in.

After about an hour five of us returned to the Wires and Lazo went up the hill and to the C section. As we were walking the Room Senior was telling us about Lazo's behavior with the Officer-in-Charge. "He's cheeky, that Lazar, he stood still for over an hour and didn't say a word. The Officer-in-Charge sent him up to the C section. A Blue Angel came to take him up the hill. A tough Slovenian, but we'll soften him up. He'll be as soft as a rabbit's tail. About those scrubbings, you'll do two of them tonight, from eight o'clock till midnight, and I'll let you know about the remaining three."

It started raining at a quarter to eight. A siren hailed for the evening recount. The rain was becoming heavier and heavier but none of us were allowed to cover ourselves with a piece of carton, a blanket or anything else. Only the Room Seniors wore brand new raincoats.

A Blue Angel forgot to note that Lazo was sent off to the C section, so one person was missing during the recount. Everything had to be double checked – we had to be counted once more. By 9:00 we were soaking wet, dripping all over. It seemed like the rain was working for the Blue Angels.

At 9:30 we were told there would be no scrubbing that night because of the rain, and we were all sent to the dormitories, which were so badly constructed that there were puddles of water all over. It was leaking through the roof and onto the beds and some of the straw beds felt like giant wet sponges. There were seventy people in one dormitory, mostly in two or three-level bunk beds.

Dear mother of God, how would I make it through the night on a bed like that!

A brigadier that slept in the room with us told us to keep quiet. He slept behind blinds in the corner. He didn't have a fixed job and could move wherever he wanted; of course this was limited to the places where convicts worked. One brigadier covered twenty-six convicts, but sometimes there weren't enough of them so they would cover up to a hundred men. Their duty was to inspect our feet at night and to oversee our work.

Brigadiers were nasty – they would never inspect our feet while we were still awake. No, they would wait about half an hour or longer, until everyone would fall asleep and then wake us all up.

"I'm not your wife to have to touch your legs. Move your legs to the side of the bed and uncover your feet so I can see them well! Will you look at this old sloppy bastard? Fifty-six years old but his feet are dirty as if he hasn't washed them in about a hundred years. Get up, you old piece of shit! Some nerve you've got to be waiting for me with such feet!"

All this came from a twenty-year-old convicted to thirteen years for murdering his mistress when she was with another man. He wasn't tired because he never really worked. The food he got was excellent and he was always dressed better than the other prisoners. He had never been beaten because he collaborated with the police and was worse than any Blue Angel. There was nothing he saw or heard that he didn't report.

One night he insulted an Albanian who later waited for him in the latrine and stabbed him three times so that he almost died.

The latrine was a very convenient place for these kinds of things to happen because there were no lights and because it was open – it had a roof but had no barriers so that forty people could use it at the same time. At night you couldn't tell who was sitting next to you. There also wasn't any toilet paper. As we weren't allowed to go anywhere without a hat, many of them would get stolen. Those who had their hats stolen would come to the latrine at night and steal somebody else's. Nobody could react fast enough while relieving himself and by the time you got dressed the hat thief would be long gone. The newcomers would often lose their hats this way.

A noise was heard. The whole Wires awoke. Two men were being carried to the surgery. Albanians made a mistake and instead of stabbing two Bosnians, which was the plan, they stabbed a man from Osijek and a man from Niš, originally a Montenegrin.

We could tell it was a revenge attack because the stab wounds were on their behinds and legs. The man from Osijek was stabbed thirteen times and the other one nine times. The Blue Angels beat the Albanians and took them to the C section by force, and then carried the wounded men to the convicts' surgery.

"My God, who can stand this mad house?"

"Try and bear it, it'll pass!"

"I'm all torn and it's three o'clock already. One more hour and then we have to get up. This is hell!"

The brigadier ordered us to go to bed. His order was the law and nobody could complain.

*Goli Otok*

## Screwed

Another monotonous day dawned with the same old scenes on the way to work. A quarter to six in the morning a member of the UDBA, employed as a technician, was working as the chief of the stone processing plant in the economic section of the press where terrazzo tiles and mosaic pieces (40x40 cm) were being made. There were two rotation presses from Italy that could pour in and mold around nine thousand pieces in eight hours, if there were no interruptions during work.

"Everyone from the big rotational press come here! Why did you mold only seven thousand pieces yesterday? Momo, you work as an engine technician, you tell me," the chief said.

"We couldn't work any faster because item five was being made and a lot of it broke. We had to work slowly because otherwise we would have destroyed a lot of material."

"Liar! The second shift was doing item five as well and they made nine thousand pieces. But that technician isn't a saboteur like you are. Today I want more than the quota. If you don't make it, you're going to the Separation until the end of your time here, is that clear? Now, get to work!"

Not even half of the quota was done by 11:00.

"Ivo, it looks like I'm going to the Separation; the work is going slow," said Momo.

"No, you aren't. I'll break the press as soon as the brigadier and that Blue Angel go away."

"Don't do that, I'll only get in trouble!"

"Don't you worry, they'll never find out why it's broken."

Ivo put a 34-millimeter screw under one of the four hammers in the hydraulic press where the terrazzo concrete was being pressed. Strong pressure and the thick screw caused the press to explode, but unfortunately we couldn't remove the screw in time because before we knew it two Blue Angels arrived after hearing the explosion. They didn't have a hard time figuring out what the cause was.

Čor was there too, "I knew it! They've been sabotaging work for two days. I want all six of them in my office!"

Momo was the first to be questioned, the rest waited outside. Two Blue Angels, Pemper and Mrki, were present at the questioning.

"Who planted the screw?" asked Čor.

"I don't know."

"You don't know, you don't know!"

Čor lifted the desk and placed its legs on a piece of wood that laid there especially for that purpose. He ordered Momo to take off his trousers and bend over the raised desk. Momo pretended not to hear Čor but then Mrki hit him on the head with a club and he fell down. The two huge Blue Angels lifted him and placed him on the desk and then beat him each from their own side. Momo soon came to, but the hits in the ribs and the stomach caused him to vomit. The door opened and Momo was thrown out of the room.

Ivo was the next one to go in. When he said he didn't know who had planted the screw, he also had to take off his trousers and bend over. He was tiny and weak so he didn't dare to hesitate. Mrki and Pemper hit his naked body with their billy clubs. After a short time he began to defecate and urinate on himself and was thrown out screaming.

"Come in, paramedic Budo. This has got to

be your idea; you're the most educated of them. You ordered them to do it, didn't you?"

"Like you said, I'm a paramedic, but putting screws in the press is not a part of medicine. What I do is take tiles out of the press and the screw was placed under the hammers. How should I know how it got there?"

"You don't say, fucking saboteur. You'll talk, but it'll be too late then. Take off your trousers!"

"Why should I?"

"You have the nerve to ask? Did you hear him? Take off his shirt, I want him completely naked!"

But Budo didn't want to, so they grabbed him, took off his clothes by force, tied his legs to the legs of the desk and his hands on the other side.

"Start talking. Who placed the screw into the press?"

He kept repeating he didn't know, so they started hitting him with the clubs.

"Beat the hell out of him," Čor said. And really, Mrki and Pemper beat him so much they crushed his genitals. His muscles were beaten like steaks and his skin was all bruised and bloody. After the beating he was sent to the prison hospital where he was treated in solitary, away from all other patients.

We were all beaten in the same way, and then it was Ivo's turn again. This time he admitted everything because he couldn't stand hearing our screams anymore, caused by the mad Blue Angels' treatment.

"What kind of a person are you? You got everyone beaten because of something you did. Who talked you into it?"

"Nobody talked me into it. I just didn't want you to send Momo to the Separation. That's why I did it."

"What's he to you?"

"He's my neighbor and a school buddy."

"Right, you're off to the C section and the others to the solitary because they didn't want to say they knew you did it."

"None of them knew anything."

"Pemper, shall I take him away or shall you?"

"No, no. I have to make some phone calls. Have Perica take him away."

Ivo demanded to see the prison warden straight away.

"You can't see him just like that," said Mrki. "You have to talk to the Officer-in-Charge first and he has to allow it. Get to work!"

"But I can't even stand up straight, let alone work. I want to see the warden!"

Mrki went to make a phone call. When he returned half an hour later he said "everyone to the solitary. The warden will visit you there and then you can talk to him. And don't you complain; you brought this on yourselves!"

*Goli Otok*

## Solitary and C Section

Two convicts saw us being brought to the solitary. They were new there from the C section where they started a hunger strike as a form of protest.

Hunger strikers were never beaten. The hospital manager was always called and he would feed them through tubes. These two men were pronounced crazy after a few days, put in straightjackets and sent to the nuthouse even though they were perfectly sane.

There were many others in the solitaries that were sent there under the suspicion of doing various things against the island's law.

I heard Radak's infamous voice: "Hey you, jerk, what are you banging for? I'm gonna kick your ass."

"It wasn't me, it was someone else," said a man from the neighboring cell.

"You're that Mišić guy who wanted the independent Croatian state without Orthodox Serbs in Lika!"

*Bam, bam, bam* followed.

"Please don't, commander! Why are you beating me? Isn't it enough that I'm chained like this and sleeping without a blanket?"

"Drop dead, you fucking son of a bitch! You want to run away from here, you piece of shit! Less than fifty kilos and you're trying to run the politics and fight us."

*Bam, bam, bam, bam* again.

"This is so you always remember who's Radak. You're in the right place now. We've beaten Marxist Leninist ideology and now here's the smart Mišić who wants to beat us. Haven't you heard? I'd beat you all and kill you if I had the power in my hands?"

After ten days in the solitary the time came for us to be moved to the C section. After distributing us to the rooms we were to scrub the 50-meter-long hallway.

"Stojan, make them scrub it nicely, the way scrubbing is done here."

Stojan was the Room Senior in the C section. He was sentenced to twelve years on the island because he had raped a sixty-year-old woman, but, being a good snitch, he got the job.

He filled ten 20-liter buckets with water and spilled it on the floor. Then he gave us each a cloth the size of a handkerchief and demonstrated how scrubbing was done in the C section. "You mustn't bend your knees and you do as you are told."

"What kind of an explanation is that?" asked Lazo.

"Stand next to each other and start . . . No, that's not the way to do it, you tall guy. You small one, climb on his back! Faster, faster . . . turn around, the end of the hallway is there. . . ."

And then the tall guy fainted. He came around after a few kicks, and again his scrubbing was no good. It was impossible to collect all that water with the pieces of cloth that we were given. The tall guy again had someone climb on his back, and again he collapsed. This time kicking couldn't bring him back so Stojan splashed a bucket of water over him.

"Take that jerk to the basement and keep him there until he comes to. And the rest of you hurry up, turn . . . faster . . . that's no good. Listen, you assholes, how long do you plan to fuck with me?!"

And so we kept scrubbing with no purpose because the hallway really wasn't dirty. We all started losing our strength, and it showed.

This was absolute insanity. Would I be able to able to bear it or would I leave my bones here like many others?

At 4:00 it was time to get up – work in the C section was never done when it was dark. The day began with an hour of floor scrubbing, then a really short time for washing our faces, and then breakfast – a tasteless farina with no or very little fat. At breakfast time we went to the dining room from the dormitory through the hallway, in a single file, and we filled the seats silently. After everyone was seated we heard an order: "Take off the hats, start!"

We stopped eating after the commands "Stop!" or "Finish!" After that we would go back to our rooms to put on our shoes and line up.

The line to the quarry was several hundred meters long and we were not allowed to say a word or turn our heads, even though there was nothing to see apart from the rocks with no grass or trees, just here and there a small hawthorne bush.

Upon arrival to the quarry the work was distributed by a convict who was given the power to do so. He also watched to see if anyone was doing anything forbidden. If he didn't like you, he assigned you to the "search" – to carry stone or soil. The quotas were so high they were nearly impossible to fill. Carrying the boxes was overseen by Blue Angels.

In eight hours 400 boxes had to be filled and carried by two men 500 meters. If a pair did five boxes less they would be forgiven. If they did fifty boxes less, they received a blow on the behind for each of them. The Blue Angel would ask you whether you wanted atomic or hydrogen blows and everyone had the right to choose. If you decided to take atomic blows, you would get a blow per missing box. Those who decided to receive hydrogen blows would get half as many, only the blows were much harder.

You took atomic blows while standing, on the way from work, and hydrogen ones bending over a chair once you returned from work. You had to count the blows yourself. If you lost the count, it would start over from the beginning. As for atomic blows, a Blue Angel would count himself.

The unlucky ones who missed more than fifty boxes had to continue working until 6 p.m. without lunch. After that, dinner, and then scrubbing until 11 p.m. as punishment. The scrubbing was harder than any work in the quarry because it had to be done in a specific body position that we were not permitted to change.

The Blue Angels often picked a man they wanted to beat up, but if they couldn't find a reason to do so, they would pair that man up with someone they persuaded to stall the work. The person would work slowly so that little work would get done and the other guy would get as many blows as possible. In such cases they would get up to fifty hydrogen blows, and when the count was up to twenty the Blue Angel would say the right number was eighteen and the beating would start from the beginning. They never agreed with the convict about the number of blows received. Mostly Croats, Herzegovinians and Albanians suffered such beatings. The other man would also receive a beating, but it wouldn't really be that hard.

A twenty-five-year-old Angel never felt any

remorse while beating a bold fifty-year-old engineer or teacher. Quite on the contrary! They would talk down and swear and insult them in any possible way. The warden approved of this procedure and you couldn't go any further than the warden to complain.

*Josip Zoretić*

# Stipe

At around 10 a.m. the next day a voice was heard from the hut: "Sweet mother of God, please don't commander, ow, ow, ow!"

Shortly after that he went silent, he couldn't even cry anymore. Lazo had beaten Stipe, a Dalmatian, convicted to twelve years for mining the railroad where Tito was supposed to pass.

After some time I saw him all dripping wet; they had poured some water over him and leaned him against a small hill to come to his senses.

Stipe didn't work anymore that day, but the next day he had to work again even though he was in no shape to do so. Lazo and plenty of Blue Angels were there and Stipe had to work like everybody else or he would get beaten again. He was too weak to even decide which of the two jobs to choose. He asked me to help him, but I was barely doing my job on the tippers that brought stone to the Separation.

"You could help me if you wanted to," Stipe said to me. "When I see you arrive with a full tipper, I'll come running and put my arm under it so that it gets broken. Once it's broken they'll have to send me to the hospital."

"Calm down Stipe, this'll pass some day. If you lose your arm, you'll never have it again, and if you try and stick it out a little bit longer, you might just survive this place."

"I don't think I can take this. Please, help me!"

"Stipe, you're working on the tippers today. We'll all help you fill the quota. I'll ask the others, don't worry."

"It's no use brother, I'm no good anymore. My ribs hurt so much I can hardly breathe. I've been pissing blood, they destroyed my kidneys."

"We have to work or the guy on the hill is going to see us talking. If you've decided to have your arm broken, I'll push the tipper as fast as I can and I'll leave the rest to you."

"I'll pretend to accidentally fall over and push my arm under the wheel. If they try to get the truth out of you, you'll know what to say. But I don't think they'll ask any questions."

"Right. And why did that guy beat you so hard?"

"I swore in front of that guy from Belgrade; I said some things about his mother and he complained to Lazo."

Twenty minutes later I was pushing the tipper and Stipe ran toward the Separation, if you could call it running, and fell next to the tipper. There was blood on the rail and on the crossties. His fingers were twitching, cut off from his hand.

"Tie off his hand so he doesn't lose too much blood, and get back to work. I'll take him to the hospital," said the guard.

I don't know what happened to Stipe after that – I never saw or heard of him again.

Six men that didn't fill the quota that day were required to report to Radaković in his building. Among them were two pilot lieutenants, a major, two students and a medical school dropout. They didn't have to go in though, because Radaković told them he would call them later. They were sleeping in my dormitory.

We couldn't tell the time because nobody had a watch. The only clock was in the C section building and sometimes we could see what time it was. At around 9:00 two door bolts slid open and the door swung open.

"Those six men come out now!"

They left the dormitory and were scrubbing from 9 to 1 a.m., and they still had to get up at 4 a.m. with the rest of us. Only their good physical shape saved them from fainting and, consequently, from a beating.

If you didn't fold your clothes properly or if you talked too loudly, you would also have to do some scrubbing at night.

The next day they were transferred to the rock drilling. You couldn't goof off there because each man had to dig a three-meter hole in eight hours. This was done in pairs and it could only be done if you worked hard. It mostly went well until about 11:00, but after that you started losing your strength. A hammer weighing seven kilograms became too heavy, especially on hot days.

There was a latrine nearby and the convicts used the opportunity to have a cigarette or two with the excuse of having to "go," but before long the Blue Angels caught on. They found a Gipsy from the Kosmet, whose only duty was to watch to see if anyone was fooling around. And he loved the job. He enjoyed looking at other people's naked butts and penises to see if they were really relieving themselves. He reported about what every single man was doing in the latrine. If someone was there doing anything else, the self-appointed judge reported it right away to the Blue Angels who would carry out the punishment without hesitation.

*Goli Otok*

# Ismet and Joja

The next day new assignments were given. The brigadier decided that Ismet and Joja would work together. Joja was a nickname he got in Spain, where he stole a jewel pronounced 'joja' (yoya) when he was in a financial crisis. He was banned from Spain after that. They were to go drill stone and Ismet accepted the job without hesitation. Joja even said "with pleasure."

The two of them were planning to escape, and not many people knew about it. At around 8:00 a strong southern wind started blowing, and a little later a thunderstorm began. Joja and Ismet disappeared in the commotion, and the police didn't imagine anyone could run away in weather like that. They thought the runaways would probably hide somewhere until the storm subsided and try to leave the island later. But, just in case, they started patrolling the coast with the speedboats. However, the speedboats had to return because of the huge waves around the island and the heavier boats had all sailed away, so the coast was really clear.

I found out about the success of their escape years later when I made it off the island and heard Ismet had a restaurant in Germany. The southern wind had carried Joja and Ismet toward the coast and they didn't even need to swim too much. The wind helped the two young men escape from the island and they eventually escaped from Yugoslavia as well. The case raised a lot of publicity on the island and shocked the police. A lieutenant-colonel punished all the policemen who were on duty in the quarry that day with twenty-five percent off their pay checks.

An unbearable iron discipline was being enforced on the island, and yet it wasn't a total success.

*Goli Otok*

# False Reports

Around noon the quarry was blown up with explosives by members of the police and an old civilian mine expert called Miha. During the explosion the convicts stood in a line near the quarry. Those who had a rougher time than the others and who couldn't stand it anymore used the opportunity to run toward the explosives and throw themselves on it, thus getting blown to pieces. The police tried to stop them but more often than not they couldn't if they were too close to the explosion site, not wanting to get too close to the explosion themselves.

The prison management would register these killed men as escaped.

Eventually, explosions no longer took place while convicts were in the quarry in order to prevent them from taking their own lives this way.

Many convicts attempted other ways to escape the daily bashing and torture, such as intentionally breaking their own bones with picks or similar tools. Many of us had never been brave enough to go as far as breaking our own bones. The management would allow the fractured parts to be put in cast and the convict wouldn't have to go to work in the quarry.

The food they got was no better than normal, but for some of them this was the only way of escaping the daily bashing. After a few days, when the pain would ease, they had to work sitting down if a leg was in a cast, or with only one arm if the other arm was in a cast. They would normally work in the kitchen or the carpentry shop, where there were various jobs.

I remember when a Slovenian was beaten on the loins. He was bloated like a frog and died because both of his kidneys were destroyed. The report, that nobody asked for anyway, said he had hanged himself.

There was also a Hungarian man who was beaten to death in the solitary, and he was reported to have died of cancer.

The law made such false reporting possible because the statute of the island said that any convict who died while serving his sentence must be buried in the convicts' cemetery. After the sentence expired, the remains could be taken to a civilian cemetery only if the president of the republic specifically allowed it, or if he pardoned the convict and allowed the remains to be transferred. But no one was ever pardoned, so relatives of any of the deceased never found out the true cause of death, let alone seeing remains or pieces of the blown-up bodies. Those were Ranković's special orders. This way Ranković, "Tito's Marko" as Tito called him, tried to intimidate the non-Serbs and their followers so that they wouldn't create any resistance once he created Greater Serbia from the Yugoslav provinces.

The island's mafia created laws that suited them. The island was well-protected; no ship was allowed to sail near it unless approved in advance. Every official was allowed to give orders to convicts, who were not allowed to disobey, even if the order was against the island's laws. As a result, some officials forced a man to perform homosexual acts just because he didn't shave well.

Many such cases were revealed later on because the officials would ask the men to clean their offices with the explanation that they had done it so well before, and later they would even ask that they be assigned to them as their secretaries or janitors.

*Goli Otok*

A lieutenant-colonel found several such cases suspicious and he tried to find out what was behind them. It was all discovered when a policeman accidentally entered an unlocked room and saw intercourse. The door had been unlocked because not just anyone was allowed to enter that room, but this time it all came out in the open. The convict told the circumstances under which he had been doing it. Soon enough they both left the island and nobody ever heard anything of them again.

*Josip Zoretić*

# Export Products

The management decided that the convicts should keep national holidays in good memory. To do so, and in order to take maximum advantage of the convicts, they organized a competition on May 1 and November 29. The competition for May 1 began on February 1 and finished on April 28. The competition in honor of the Day of the Republic, the most important of Yugoslav public holidays, started on September 1 and lasted until November 25. During this period there wasn't a day off for anyone.

Each year the competition involved production – the prisoners were to make as many chairs as possible – and it would take place after regular work. We worked on machines for twelve hours a day and nobody was spared. There were no night shifts on those days.

The chairs, which were being sold on the American market, left the island with the label *Velebit Rijeka Industrial Conglomerate* – the same label as the terrazzo tiles.

Everybody had to take part in the competition. Food was given to us during the competition and there were no lunch or dinner breaks – food was handed out to us one at a time since having a break would have spoiled the spirit of the competition. Only those in the C section didn't compete with the rest, they had to supply stone for the Concreting and cheap stone for sale that was taken away on ships.

The top ten competitors won mostly books, but old and used books that were not of any interest to anyone on the outside.

There were those who declined to compete, but they weren't beaten for it. Instead, they would be treated horribly every time we went to work. They had to carry up to twenty-five kilograms of heavy stone from the Wires entrance to the stone processing plant. The walk was difficult and about two and a half kilometers long, and the haranguer that had refused to compete wasn't allowed to have himself replaced for a moment.

Sometimes their hands would go weak but they weren't allowed to go any faster or slower than the file. The Blue Angels would stop the file and tie the person's hands to the handles of the carrier so that they wouldn't slip off. The file would then be sent forward, faster than before, in order to make up for lost time.

When we were finally in the plant they had to work as if their hands were in perfect order. Their defiance only lasted several days. After feeling the consequences they soon joined the rest and competed without saying a word.

*Josip Zoretić*

## Sabotage

The convicts hated the island and the state immensely, so attempts to sabotage were not uncommon.

In the stone processing plant there were grinding and milling machines – huge machines used for grinding tiles and stone. They ran on electricity and plenty could be done with them. As soon as the brigadier or a Blue Angel turned away a convict would try to do something, while at the same time making sure that the sabotage wasn't discovered.

Water was used during the grinding process and it provided a useful tool to damage the electric machines. Normally we would pour water into the electric motors because it was easily done, but it was always done with great care, making sure that nobody who would report us was watching.

The machines were built in such a way that the transmission belts were in a vertical position, so pouring water in was easy. The engines had more than one electric motor in them, so if we poured water into one that was not working while the other one was engaged, you couldn't tell anything was wrong by the sound of it alone. But when the watered motor was turned on it had to be taken out because it malfunctioned.

The break never lasted long because a spare motor was fitted, and the electrician said it was humidity that had caused the motors to malfunction. His words were taken for granted because he was a member of the UDBA. Such things were done for the sake of revenge, even though not much was really accomplished.

*Goli Otok*

## Escape

"Hey Josip, that four-eyes from the C section sent you this letter. I'm sure you recognize his handwriting."

"I beg you, if you can, could you get me some of those blades for the hacksaw? The blacksmith will smuggle them into the building. Don't you worry no one will catch you. Your friend Edo" said the note.

It wasn't easy to smuggle because of the strict control by the police and it took several days to make the delivery.

The blacksmith wasn't in the C section as some sort of punishment but was there working, repairing pickaxes, shovels and other similar tools. He could get in and out of the C section without being searched. He was playing both sides of the street – of the police and of some convicts he chose.

A locksmith obtained the hacksaws and they were taken to an agreed location. Three men were involved in taking the hacksaws to the place where the blacksmith would later pick them up on his way from work.

"It's done," I heard from the man who was the last one involved in the delivery. The saws were intended to cut the window bars in Edo's dormitory.

After the hard work in the quarry everyone could hardly wait to lie down and rest. Everyone was sleeping like a log apart from the three men who wrapped one half of the blade in a piece of cloth and were sawing the window bars. They worked in shifts so that someone was always on the lookout, watching to see if someone would notice and report what they were doing. Maybe someone even heard them, but nobody reported them. The building was such that no one had ever succeeded in breaking out of it, so the policemen never guarded the dormitories in it, only the basement where the solitaries were located. Upstairs the guard on duty was in his office by the phone.

That night the three men successfully cut the bars, tied the bed sheets one to another and climbed down the outside wall. They had rolled up some blankets, put them on their beds and covered them with one more blanket, so that when the guard on duty was checking the rooms through the peepholes he wouldn't be suspicious.

When their escape was discovered in the morning it was already too late. All three men were far away from the island. Had they not escaped, Edo would have had eight more years to serve, the other two men five years each.

This was a large blunder by the police, so they decided to immediately replace all the window bars with stronger ones. The old bars were just regular bars yet nobody had ever managed to cut them up until then. The hacksaw blades were also found, but it was never discovered how they got to the dormitory.

All this boosted the morale of the convicts but at the same time brought certain drawbacks to the iron discipline that was already being enforced, which then became even worse. Prior to this incident nobody ever used to examine our genitals, now they started doing that as well, using gloves of course. Yet the morale was boosted; it was a victory over Ranković's men. Many men realized nothing was impossible and many escape attempts ensued despite the fact that the waters around Goli Otok were patrolled. Whoever got caught swimming was said to have drowned. Only very few ever managed to swim across the Senj Channel.

One convict, a Kosovar Albanian named Makoli, was also preparing to escape. He asked for help from his fellow countryman whose job was driving crane trucks and forklifts called *Indos*. As Makoli had twelve more years to serve, he decided to take a chance and planned the getaway with his fellow countryman.

In the hope of getting his sentence reduced his countryman was collaborating with the police, which was the reason his job was no more than driving. However, Makoli was obviously too stupid to have realized it. He counted on the driver to give him the inner tires for safer swimming, which he did, just as he made him a nicely polished knife as big as a bayonet.

Makoli decided to escape from the Wires on a stormy night because during such weather there were often problems with the power supply and blackouts were not uncommon. He wrapped the tires around him in the driver's workshop and hid the knife in his trousers. The driver had previously told the lieutenant-colonel, who gave orders to the Blue Angels, not to watch what Makoli was doing from 2 to 2:15, during which time he was wrapping himself up in tires and hiding the knife. The driver was also to be hidden so that nobody would figure out that he was the one who reported him because the Albanians would kill him for it. Everything was being prepared in the vehicle repair workshop where there was nobody else except for the driver; others who worked there were all busy driving out in the plant.

*Josip Zoretić*

The lieutenant-colonel ordered that everyone be examined thoroughly. The file in front of ours was coming from the carpentry shop and two small knives were found on them. Our file was coming from behind the control building and when we noticed that the other file was being searched we started throwing away the knives that we had on us. Two Blue Angels were at the back of the file for the very purpose of seeing if anyone would throw anything away. As the file was very long they couldn't see much, the road being full of curves with walls on one end and rocks on the other. Somebody at the front of the file said through a tissue: "Fire!" ["*Vatra!*"] This was a signal of danger from the search and everyone down the line immediately got rid of whatever forbidden objects they had. The leaders of the file saw some things being thrown away but all hands looked alike and all our suits were alike and no one wore rings. Wearing rings was forbidden because rings could be sold, if anyone managed to escape from the island, to buy a bus ticket or, what was even more important, civilian clothes.

No one was caught red-handed, so some men were later beaten to confess to throwing things away.

There was nothing Makoli could do to get rid of his knife because it was stuck in his trousers, and there was absolutely no way he could get rid of the tires wrapped around his chest.

There were around seventy policemen at the gate and several of them lay in the rocks, armed, so that they could shoot in case of a fight. Some were also standing along the road with trained dogs and they could intervene as well, if necessary.

## Goli Otok

The file came to the cutting that led to the gate, where there were supporting walls on both sides, built by the Cominform. The file hadn't even reached the gate when a lieutenant ordered us to raise our hands and keep still. We all obeyed. The file of four spaced off and the search began, three Blue Angels per file. The lieutenant-colonel was standing on the second floor of the watchtower, next to him a Blue Angel holding a machine gun, its barrel sticking out so that it would have the desired psychological effect on the convicts.

The search wasn't all that thorough because the two men who were leading the file said that any blades had already been thrown away; it was obvious they were looking for one person in particular. Makoli was somewhere in the middle of the file, second from the right. Two officers were searching together; the third one was further away. When the two officers got to Makoli they went straight for his bosom, where the tires were hidden. They stripped him naked and found the knife and a metal file. They then grabbed him from behind by the neck and banged his head against the wall, but that didn't kill him; he lay on the ground and they started kicking and treading on him. When they finally had enough they left him to be watched by the dogs, which was not a problem for the dogs since he wasn't moving at all. He was hardly breathing. The dogs followed the lieutenant's order: one holding him by a leg and the other by the chest. Another order followed, which was directed at us: "Forward, bastards!" and the file entered the Wires. The police didn't want to lynch Makoli publicly, so he survived but with severe consequences.

It couldn't be found out who had snitched on Makoli until he recovered from his injuries. He remained in the C section, and yet he managed to pass the information out that his fellow countryman betrayed him. Once he realized the Albanians would take revenge on him and kill him, the driver asked for police protection. In order to save his life the lieutenant-colonel shortened his sentence by one year and had him transferred to another prison. He had four more years to serve, but nobody could fine out which correctional institution he had been sent to.

The convicts continued attempting whatever they could to get away. The police used all their expertise and placed one convict outside each pavilion to keep guard. Even though a counting took place every half hour, which was done by three police officers together, people kept trying to escape.

Convicts M. and S.T. managed to leave the island during a storm when the power was out. While they were at sea the wind and the waves wouldn't carry them away but instead kept bringing them back, along with two planks that they used that were probably left there the last time someone tried to escape. The planks started to sink and the merciless waves wouldn't let the men move away from the island. As the storm and rain kept raging the convict on duty noticed two men were missing and reported it to the police. Much to their misfortune, M. and S.T. had to return to the Wires. They were allowed to go to bed. Around that time the power was back on, and so were the police who came for them.

"Where the hell have you two been? Surely in the latrine. And who cut the wire behind it while it was dark? And which way did you return? We were watching everything. Don't you lie, now rush to the Center!"

Convict M. received 200 blows with a billy club in his wet clothes, which the police officers found extremely satisfying because the suits were thin and they stuck to the skin so the billy clubs practically hit the skin itself. He didn't want to confess to the getaway attempt. Convict S.T. received 170 blows. They were both treated in the prison clinic where they remained for twenty days, after which they were transferred to the C section. They were lucky that those three Blue Angels were at the Center at that time because at other times there was one there who took extreme pleasure in hearing the sound of his billy club.

They remained in the C section for six months and then they were returned to the Wires.

Summer was not a particularly good time for attempting an escape. The water is warm then and the speedboats never stopped patrolling the waters around the island. It was the cold season that was more suitable because the water was thought to be too cold for anyone to swim. Fugitives somehow found a way to diminish the suffering of low water temperatures; they applied various greasy matters onto their skin such as machine oil, waste hydraulic fluid or anything similar they could get hold of. This was the only possible way of insulating the body, but more often than not it wasn't sufficient protection. If they were discovered swimming they would be drowned, smothered or simply shot. Some were even run over by speedboats if the patrol felt like doing so. Some men managed to get past the island patrol, but then they were caught by the coast patrols.

*Josip Zoretić*

There was once the case of a Hungarian aircraft mechanic, F., who managed to swim a good distance away from the island before the police noticed he was gone and radioed to the nearby patrols that they were to help recapture him. Fugitive F. was caught near the town of Senj by the regular police and held in custody until the island police officers came to take him back. They weren't allowed to dispose of him though, because the regular police filed a report saying he was in good health upon being handed over to the island police.

He was first taken by police vehicle to the shore and then placed on a speedboat. They took the long way so as to torture F. a little longer. He was thrown into the water and pushed under the surface, just long enough for him not to drown. When that was done his clothes were taken off and his genitals were tied with a rope that was pulled by the boat. His genitals surprisingly didn't come off but they just barely stayed attached to his body. Lieutenant Nikolić had directed this scene. The beating followed later on in the C section solitary.

*Goli Otok*

# The Dead Fund

There was no such thing as a salary on the island; instead, we received reward money, up to 5000 dinars a month. We never actually received this money; accounts were kept in a bank book. The highest amounts would usually be paid to Room Seniors and brigadiers; others generally received 1800 dinars. The highest reward amount in the C section was 800 dinars a month.

Two-thirds of the total was paid into the convict's bank book and could be used to buy razors, soap, toothpaste, canned food, sugar, orange juice and various Yugoslav cigarettes in the convicts' shop, which was run by a civilian member of the UDBA. A small 100-gram can of food cost 195 dinars, a half-bottle of orange juice was as much as 400 dinars, and sugar was 180 dinars per kilogram. The mildest cigarettes, *Drava*, cost 120 dinars per pack. Sometimes I would buy cigarettes to trade for sugar.

The last third of the money was used for the so-called *Dead Fund*; that is to say, it was used to pay for our burial in case we died on Goli Otok. Not that the burial cost all that much, but we had to save for it nonetheless. Whenever somebody died they would just be wrapped in a bed sheet and placed in a hole that was dug as deep as the rocky ground allowed. There would be some chlorine and lime placed over it and then it would be covered with rocks. The *Dead Fund* existed also as a place to save all the money that was sent to a convict by his family, and it would stay there until the day one left the island or died.

*Josip Zoretić*

# Journalists

In an attempt to hide all the horrible things that were going on on Goli Otok, deputy warden Radoslav Runko invited journalists from Zagreb to visit the island and write about it. Needless to say, the journalists never spoke to a single convict. They just wrote what the island officials told them and described what they saw. But, what they saw was a real show.

The day before their arrival orders were given through the loudspeakers in every dormitory. Half of the men didn't have to work that day, they could rest if they wanted to, both in the Wires and in the C section. The food was suddenly excellent, not even the rich could have asked for something tastier. The game room was open and chess was played all day long. Even the cinema announced a film would be on in the evening.

The cinema was run by one of the convicts and was built by the convicts after their regular working hours. Sometimes a film would be shown but not just anyone could see it. We could only enter if we had tickets and they were given away by a Room Senior, a brigadier or a police officer. The programs were bad: *Ivan the Terrible, The Ploughed Up Wasteland*, Russian and Yugoslav propaganda films and other crap that no one outside the island wanted to see. They were played at night only because the daytime was reserved for work. We were all counted upon entering the cinema and were supposed to go straight to our dormitories after the film was over, but as I said, not everyone was allowed this kind of entertainment.

Runko showed it all to the journalists and it didn't seem bad at all. Some pictures were taken for the newspaper and gave the impression that spending time on Goli Otok was like being on vacation, that we had nothing to do.

Runko even wrote a booklet with the title *What is a Billy Club on Goli Otok*, full of propaganda and lies. He gave several copies to the island library, and from time to time asked the convicts how they found it, with a grin on his face, of course. He often used to say: "You are not aware of the horrible things you have done, but the law got to you. You have forced our management to introduce a special regime different from all other regimes in other correctional institutions in Yugoslavia."

*Josip Zoretić*

# Vinko

A convict named Vinko M. was appointed brigadier in charge of a group of men working on loading and unloading ships. They had to work whenever was necessary – day or night. Vinko was authorized to lead the convicts from the dormitory in the Wires to the dock where the ships landed, delivering wood and large amounts of cement. The police took over at the dock.

Persuaded by some fellow convicts, he agreed to lead a group of men through the gate. It was on a Sunday evening when a large number of the police officers were in the police hotel drinking. Also, the guard on duty at the gate never suspected such a good brigadier would be up to something.

Vinko decided to help steal the fastest speedboat with his men – the same boat the police used to patrol around the island. There was nobody outside the Wires that night, nobody was working and the police officer on the dock didn't pay much attention to the anchored ship – he was in his watchtower, reading the newspaper, while the ship's crew was having fun in the police hotel.

What Vinko was about to do was very dangerous but he was the only one who knew his way around the dock and the situation there, and he knew all the officers. He kept encouraging the others who not for a second forgot about the bullets that could hit them if something went wrong.

The speedboat was locked in its compartment, surrounded by concrete walls from all sides, with a strong iron door secured with a suspended padlock produced especially in Hungary. There were two more compartments secured in the same way. Vinko was prepared and brought with him cutters that were strong enough to cut the padlock. He cut the padlock himself. He then helped others embark and told them not to start the motor until they were at least two kilometers away from the dock.

The foggy night helped a lot. The officer on duty couldn't see very far, yet the fact that the police weren't as alert as always was not to be underestimated. They were cautious enough to have taken out some motor parts without which the boat couldn't be started, but not cautious enough, leaving a pair of oars behind.

Our men got safely to the island of Rab where they smashed the boat and filled it with rocks until it sank to the bottom of the sea. But this was still not the end of all danger; they had to leave that island as well. Although it is an island with civilian inhabitants, there were many intelligence agents there. The entire population of Rab was constantly fed with information that the people on Goli Otok were hard-core criminals and didn't deserve to live, and that the Yugoslav government was doing them a favor by separating them from the rest of society. This rhetoric worked very well, the people believed every word of it. Whenever they saw someone wearing clothes that were not common on Rab, they would react. And the uniforms from Goli Otok stuck out.

Vinko and his companions were headed for the point which was the closest to the mainland, with the intention of leaving Rab by morning and getting to Velebit Mountain if possible.

The clock struck midnight and back on Goli Otok the guard was relieved. It was the new guard who noticed that a speedboat was missing. Long before that it was noticed that five men were missing from the Wires, and by now it was no secret who they were. After searching for them from 9 p.m. to midnight and reporting that the speedboat had been stolen, it was quite clear to everyone that they had succeeded in leaving the island. The police knew that the boat couldn't be started so they assumed the convicts hadn't gotten very far and alerted nearby police stations.

At around 3 a.m. the men were on the mainland but they ran into a police patrol that was helping the island police. There was nowhere to run and they were recaptured and brought back to the island, where they faced severe consequences. Vinko, the warden's former pet, had the hardest time and in the end lost his mind from all the torturing.

*Goli Otok*

## Power

The lieutenant-colonel realized that the police couldn't find out important information on their own so he asked that some convicts be hired to help stop the getaway attempts. These hirelings went to work on their own and at least half an hour earlier than the rest. They were mostly Serbs doing easier jobs in the warehouses. They were free to walk around the island whenever they felt like it and for as long as they wanted to.

Although this tactic proved very efficient, human conscience proved greater than any idea on the part of the police. Regardless of the nationalist and xenophobic attitudes, there were some among the hirelings who didn't approve of such police actions and who too sought to disparage the raging mafia that knew everyone and everything, just not about humaneness or feelings.

One night the power that came via underwater cables from Stari Grad to Goli Otok, and from there to Rab, went out. The cause of the power failure was unknown, so the police increased security measures and nobody was allowed to leave their dormitories. It took no less than three days before the power was back on.

Preparations were being made to work on large amounts of stone. Power Industry Rijeka couldn't find the cause of the power failure, but said that a cable must have broken somewhere under water and had to be replaced. The UDBA didn't agree and instead asked for a radar from Zagreb, which would help determine the cause.

An engineer arrived and found a cable dug out on the island, the insulation cut through. The rain that night came into contact with the cable and caused the problem. The engineer did his job well and the power didn't kill him. He repaired the cable and covered it with some rocks, so that one couldn't tell there was anything underneath.

Several hours passed before the power was switched back on in the transformer station in Stari Grad, but there was no change; something was still wrong. They then took the radar and searched on the sea, but high waves made them return. They had to try again the next day.

It turned out that the ones who caused the cable malfunction did it with great expertise – they cut the cable twice, three meters apart, and disguised it well. This could only have been done by the convicts that had freedom of movement because the rest of us always had to go to work and back silently and in a file under the strict control of Blue Angels. This showed that even those that had some freedom didn't like how the police acted.

Realizing that giving freedom to some was a wrong move, the lieutenant-colonel reversed his decision to allow freedom of movement. Now nobody had any privileges anymore. He also asked for police reinforcements, which soon arrived, but the new policemen were mainly from the passive Yugoslav republics. Even though they were supposed to do a course first, they assumed their duties straight away. They merely followed the instructions from their more experienced colleagues. They beat us harder and more often and watched every step we made. Quite often they wouldn't even let us go to the latrine. But all this didn't stop the convicts from further actions; they continued trying to undermine the police even though there was little to be gained by it.

## Tiles

Convict Milan G. was very meticulously trying to find a way to take his revenge for the beating he suffered after he once forgot to put on his cap. He knew that the only way to meet force was with force, but he was in no position to do it. Instead of conforming he started asking his friends for ideas of how to get his revenge.

He didn't know much about terrazzo tiles or about the concrete used for making them. He was educated to be a print worker. The police were well aware of his education and yet his job on the island was working with a concrete mixer, which mixed on average forty cubic meters of concrete in an eight-hour shift. This gave him a great opportunity for payback, which he never expected.

One day he was talking to a mason and mentioned his job. The mason gave him some instructions: sea water mustn't be used for making concrete because the salt in it stops the concrete from merging. This was all he needed to hear.

The concrete mixer was fitted with a pump that pumped both fresh and salt water. Supplying the whole island with fresh water was quite problematic and this had to be saved in every possible way, so salt water was brought for washing the machines after the work was done.

Milan used salt water to make concrete two days in a row without anyone noticing it, and so took his revenge for the unnecessary beating he suffered. These terrazzo tiles were supposed to be left untouched for at least twelve days before they could be ground. Of course, Milan's tiles couldn't be ground; instead they crumbled under the tumblers of sophisticated Italian *Longinotti* and *Carcano* grinders.

Civilian UDBA members, the Bosses, realized why it had happened but there was not much they could do, so they sent the tiles to a building institute in Ljubljana for analysis. It proved that there was too much salt in the material, but there was no way to prove who had committed the sabotage because two machines and many presses were used in making tiles. What made matters even more complex was that not much attention was paid when the tiles were being taken to dry. Nobody even knew when they were made.

A concrete factory was called and asked to send their own experts to analyze the concrete, but by the time they arrived at the island all the tiles had already been thrown to the bottom of the sea and many working hours were lost.

Everyone who looked even the least bit suspicious was sent to the C section and interrogated, but with no result. It was apparent that there were many among the convicts who weren't traitors and couldn't be bought with a promotion to brigadier or with freedom of movement.

Every success on part of the convicts was punished doubly by the police. In order to make up for the loss of the tiles, working on Sundays was falsified in the reports. We were told: "We're going to work Sundays to make up for what some bandits have done."

Exhausted convicts even believed that it was our own fault that we were treated so badly. They even started to believe the horrible lies coming from the police. After a while it was clear that there was no difference between working willingly and following orders.

*Goli Otok*

# Lawless

Old officials were leaving and new ones were arriving. The new officials who showed their hatred for the convicts soon found their true friends among the other officials. They could be distinguished from the others because they had their own cars, bought with the money made by convicts' extra hours work. Although such cases were forbidden by Tito's laws, the lack of control by the authorities enabled many manipulations. The only control of Goli Otok was done by Ranković and his hirelings, helpers in achieving Greater Serbia. They often took various materials from the island such as cement, electrical fittings, chairs, iron, concrete blocks, paint, and tools of all kinds. They took it for free and filed it as used up. They would say on the outside that they had bought it on Goli Otok because, apparently, they were hard to find elsewhere, which was absolutely not true.

Mirko Čor, an UDBA member, loaded several smaller ships with cement and other materials on Sundays and sold it outside for less than it normally cost.

Saturdays and Sundays were the best days for stealing this way because Fridays at 2 p.m. most officials left the island. Only one official was left in charge of about every one hundred convicts and just enough armed members of the police to maintain order in case of a riot, plus those that led the convicts to work. In other words, the island was practically left unguarded. Čor and other sophisticated thieves from the UDBA were in a position to rake in money without being suspected.

The policemen that led the convicts to work

were to oversee the work and watch for escape attempts, but were not allowed to interfere with anything the UDBA was doing; they were just to follow their orders. A few cases of such thefts were discovered and those that committed them were fired for incompetence but managed to find new jobs outside the island without any difficulty.

In the seven years that I spent on Goli Otok, Mirko Čor never got caught while making himself rich in this very clever way. He was the worst of all, in the eyes of the convicts, because nobody was as keen on ordering violent punishments, and the warden felt he was the fittest to complete his mission. If he had it in his mind to ruin someone completely, he would send them to the Separation or, even worse, to the aluminum polishing shop in the C section, for up to two years. Protection from dust particles was impossible and after six months there men would almost regularly get spots on their lungs but couldn't be transferred to another working place before the lungs started bleeding. Working conditions were beyond Čor's control but the choice of men who worked there was entirely up to him.

Treatment for tuberculosis was provided only to those who already had open caverns even though, according to an international charter, the treatment was supposed to be provided to all who needed it, be it a convict or a government minister. But Goli Otok was a place where no laws existed, only the will of the ruling sadists was enforced.

*Goli Otok*

## Existence

The UDBA member in charge of food bought huge amounts of cabbage in the autumn, which was then pickled in large concrete pools waxed with paraffin. Once the pools were filled, nobody was in charge of their maintenance. As the cabbage pickled the liquid covered the pool. Many rats would fall in, drown and eventually rot, and would stay there from autumn or winter until April, when it was served to us.

Bacon was also bought at a low price and the quality was almost always bad, but at least it was all cooked before serving and the bugs were killed – but we could still sense it all in our stomachs.

Starving convicts had no choice but to eat what they got – it was either that or nothing. If you found a rat tail and complained, you would hear, "you don't have to eat if you don't want to. Who invited you here?!"

Stomach problems were common but when medical help was asked for it was rarely received. Seeing a doctor or "going to the physical," as we called it, was only possible if you asked for it at work. The doctor never wanted to prescribe expensive medicine paid from the prison budget. Convicts were again viewed and treated as worthless scum.

The poor food worried many convicts, especially the smokers and those that had no one to send them a package from time to time or to come and visit them. We were allowed to receive a five kilogram package once every two months if we hadn't been punished by our Officer-in-Charge. Heavier packages would be returned to the sender. The warden never interfered with these regulations. Visitors were allowed to come once a month, but in those months packages were not allowed; it was either one or the other, the choice was ours.

Discussing Goli Otok was strictly forbidden during a visit. If someone mentioned anything about it, a member of the UDBA would terminate the conversation and the consequences were known to everyone. All the rooms were supervised by the police and no letters or other written messages were allowed to be exchanged. The desks in the visiting rooms were separated by plywood, so that nobody could give the other person anything under the desk; whatever was going on above the desk was easily seen by the supervisor.

A large number of men were not allowed any contact with the people on the outside and sometimes nobody even knew where they were, on Goli Otok or anywhere else, or if they were even alive. Such men were mostly placed in the C section. If they somehow succeeded in sending out news about their whereabouts to their wife or children, they still couldn't see them if they visited. The police would ask who had told them that they were on the island and play dumb, sending the visitors back with the explanation that there was no such person on Goli Otok.

As for me, I was permitted to receive a single package up to ten kilograms one week before or after May 1 or November 29. I only received one package and three visits from family in my seven years on Goli Otok. My sister Katica visited me twice and my brother Marko visited me once. Twice packages were returned; once because my sister Katica had visited. The second package was returned because I didn't show up for overtime. I didn't show up because I went to see the prison doctor, who insisted I was making up an excuse to see him.

Everyone had to take care of their hygiene in the Wires, and in the C section one had to have a haircut once every two weeks.

Shaving was something the convicts had to take care of themselves. The shaving kit was guarded by the police in a separate room and no razors were allowed in the dormitories.

The jobs we had were dirty and water supplies were limited. We couldn't even get enough salt water to wash off the dirt. Mud layers on the skin caused open wounds and blisters, especially on the more exposed areas. Treatment was made available only at a point when it was clear that the condition wasn't going to go away on its own.

Sometimes even the doctors were afraid of touching the wounds when the ones with real cause of fear were the innocent convicts who were forced to work endless hours hungry and thirsty, who were beaten, and who saw no other way out but to take matters into their own hands (or sometimes even to take their own lives).

Short-term relief for some came from making syringes and injecting chemicals, mostly petrol, into the muscles, arms, legs or wherever was possible. The reaction to the injected petrol was quite serious; the tissue would start falling apart and wounds would open that were hard to heal and stank so much one had a feeling the entire body was rotting. It only took ten drops of petrol to cause such wounds. Many injected minute amounts in many places so it looked as if the wounds were caused by dirt. Those hoping for a short break from work practiced injecting saliva which caused minor reactions.

At the very beginning it was difficult to find

out which wounds and blisters were caused by dirt and which were self-induced, so the doctors would wait for the condition to develop to a stage at which it was possible to distinguish them. Those that induced their wounds themselves were treated separately and punished for it. Those whose wounds couldn't be accounted for were allowed to recover outside the C section and weren't beaten.

The only way to prove that the wounds were caused by petrol was the strong smell they produced. Laboratory technicians working on discovering such cases couldn't do much because the laboratory wasn't properly equipped to allow diagnosing almost any disease. Doctors barely knew their jobs since they were really only police officers who, so to speak, walked through medical school and got their degrees on the way out. All the tuition expenses were paid by the state and it was of no interest to the state to fail them.

Their hearts were made of stone. They kept the shattered men locked up in a room for a day or two and only after seeing they weren't going to die would they send them to a surgeon in Rijeka or to a prison hospital in Zagreb.

I remember a convict who was trying to lift a heavy rock when something cracked inside him. He was sent to Beladinović, the hospital manager, to be examined.

"What's wrong with you?" asked Beladinović.

"I don't know. Something just snapped inside me. Something's very wrong," the convict just barely managed to say.

"It's your fucking head that's wrong! You don't feel like working, do you, so you're making things up . . . "

The patient was nevertheless examined and a

hernia was diagnosed. He had to wait three days before being sent away to have surgery, and he was lucky for being sent to have one at all. As he still had five years to serve this was the only way he could be made useful again.

*Josip Zoretić*

## Soccer

"Just look at those beasts, Milan. Look at how they're treating us."

"Well, if I had the power I'd be much worse. You've seen how many convicts hurt themselves on purpose. But never mind that now. You know what I heard from Mrki? He said that on Sunday the power transformer is going to be overhauled, so there'll be no power and we won't have to work."

"That would be great! There's a soccer match at four on the radio. Red Star from Belgrade is playing against Dinamo from Zagreb. And with the overhaul going on we'll probably be allowed to listen to the match. So tomorrow is a regular working day but after that, well, I could use a day off. I can barely walk, I'm that tired. I just wish it were true."

It really was true.

Sunday arrived and the eager fans of both the teams counted the minutes before the beginning of the match. They started gathering around the dormitory loudspeakers, the same loudspeakers that played the sounds of Radio Zagreb and that announced the police's orders or orders given by the correctional facility. The fans of Red Star, the Serbs, were on one side, the fans of Dinamo, mostly Croats, on the other.

The power arrived at around 3:00. Radio Zagreb was playing popular songs.

"Listen, Tunja, you won't be having much fun today. Justice is going to happen in Belgrade," said a Red Star fan to the Dinamo fan who, throughout all his difficult times on the island, never forgot his Dinamo, the club he adored.

"Dream on, Dušan. It might be possible if we weren't Croatian . . . "

"So what if you're from Zagreb," Dušan said scornfully. "Remember, it was you guys who found those faggots that were looking all around Belgrade for that thing that women want. You mean to beat Red Star?"

"Of course that's what we mean. And that's what we'll do. Listen, Dušan, you motherfucker, do you want to make a bet?"

"No problem! What's at stake? How about a kilo of sugar?"

"Well, I'm running a little low on it but I'll take the bet. Now we just have to find someone to hold the sugar for us until we know the winner."

"Oto, here, you take care of the sugar, please. This is mine and here comes Tunja with his. Tunja wins even if the game ends in a draw since Dinamo is a guest team. So, when the game is finished you give the sugar to the one who wins the bet. Okay?"

"Okay."

"How long before the game starts?"

"Around thirty minutes."

"Less," said a brigadier after he looked at his wristwatch. "It's 3:50."

"Hey you Dinamo fans, how come you're so quiet? I guess you know what's coming up! Serbian boys are looking at you, their mother Serbia is what they're faithful to . . . "

"Fucking assholes, I'll show you what it means to be a Dinamo fan . . . "

Several more such "compliments" were exchanged between both sides before someone interrupted them: "Quiet now, the game is about to start!"

A voice was heard from the loudspeaker: "This is Radio Zagreb. Next up is the sports afternoon. We are bringing you a live broadcast from the Marakana stadium in Belgrade where Red Star will be playing against Dinamo from Zagreb. Ivan Tomić is the commentator. You will also be able to hear reports from other games of the first national league, and at the end of the broadcast the reports from the second league games."

Some music was played and then the voice was heard again: "We're going to Belgrade now where Ivan Tomić is waiting for us . . . "

After several exciting actions on both halves, Red Star scores in the fifteenth minute of the game. All its fans were ecstatic.

"I knew it! They're so much better! Dinamo never needed to go there anyway!"

Dinamo fans are a bit sad. "It's just the beginning," they say. "There's still time."

In the thirty-eighth minute Dinamo scores even. Now it's their fans who are ecstatic. Tunja even starts to cry for joy, and someone from outside the building shouts "That's it, take them, fuck those Cyrillic bastards so they know what it means to be Croatian! Croats aren't scared, not even in Belgrade!"

Somebody from the crowd reacted with "You wanna repeat that, motherfucker?!" and a fight broke out. The police noticed it right away and when the convicts saw them coming they all disappeared so as not to let them know what the fight was about, or else the radio would be turned off.

Dinamo scored another goal in the second half and was now leading 2 to 1. There was joy among the Croats, Serbs and Croats offended each other, but there was no more fighting because the police officers were walking around.

A few minutes before the final whistle Red Star scored for the second time and the final result was 2 to 2. Dinamo fans gathered on one side to comment on the match, Red Star fans on the other. Tunja got his sugar.

A man from Zagreb passed by and asked "Hey guys, have a fag? Haven't had one since lunch and I had to wangle it out. You know, I'm somehow glad that the points are split in the game."

"I'll give you a cigarette," said one of the convicts, "but don't tell anyone where you got it or the others will start coming to me as well."

"No problem, I won't tell anyone."

"Right then, here you go. You're from Zagreb, aren't you?"

"Sure I am. What, did you think I was from Niš and supporting Dinamo? No, I'm from Zagreb, the borough of Naumovac. How much more time have you got to do here?"

"Two chunks and three meters." We called a year a chunk and a month a meter.

"That much? How come?"

"It should have been more but the sentence was shortened."

"And why are you here?"

"I was learning to do a trade. I didn't have a dime so I started picking pockets. I once earned a wallet with a grand in it. And I got it from a lawyer and he didn't notice it, so from then on I was in that line of business."

"Right, gotta go now," he said. His eyes scanned the surroundings for policemen and he left.

A little further away a man was sitting on a rock, deep in his thoughts. "What's the matter, Drnda, are you still thinking about the Belgrade draw? True, we could really have beaten those Zagreb faggots," I overheard.

"Oh fuck soccer! There they are making money. I don't see why I should worry about them; I have enough to worry about as it is."

He then went on to tell his life story.

"My parents abandoned me after the war and I don't even know who I am. I went from one shelter to another and I have no idea what parents are; no one's ever said a nice word to me. From there I was transferred to a children's home, and you know what it's like there – nobody ever tells you what's right and what's wrong. Then, when I finished school, I had to leave the home and I went to Belgrade. I thought I'd find some friends there, somebody kind. But before I knew it I was involved in crime and here I am! I got another indictment for lifting some pants at Belgrade market. I grabbed a bundle of them and ran like hell but they were after me. I ditched them in my room but the fucking landlady snitched me to the cops."

"Don't you worry, buddy. So, do you know when the trial should take place? You should get out of here before that."

"No way, I want to get back on track, have a normal life some day."

"Yeah right. Once a thief, always a thief. You guys believe you can make a living out of stealing for the rest of your lives."

"You fucking leave me alone, okay?"

A Bosnian guy came along and said to Drnda, "Are you nuts talking to him? He's a political, he hates us thieves even though they're more stupid than us. Now, if I knew a rib of mine was willing to work, or an eye for that matter, I'd have it taken out right away. Fucking work, that's what I say. I'm gonna steal for as long as I can. You do whatever you like."

"Well I'm not stealing again."

"Right. And pigs will fly!" And off went the Bosnian.

Sports were a popular subject of conversation that night. The convicts were all in a good mood because they were rested.

*Josip Zoretić*

# Elerko

A Blue Angel came by looking for Elerko, an engineer from Priština, Kosovo. When he found him he told him to accompany him to the cinema because something was apparently broken there and they needed him to fix it. The officer on duty was an UDBA member who, surprisingly, wasn't in favor of the police. He was also originally from Priština, but nobody knew when exactly the two men had met. At that time he was living in Rijeka with his wife and children.

Elerko went to repair the movie projector so that the UDBA members and members of the police could watch *Mein Kampf*, a German movie made according to Hitler's book. There was nothing seriously wrong with the projector. The UDBA member broke the thing himself in order to see Elerko in private. As soon as the Blue Angel brought Elerko, the Angel was sent away.

"As soon as we're done here I'll let you know and someone will take him back to the Wires. I take full responsibility. You may go now," he said to the Blue Angel.

There was a phone installed in the UDBA member's office and Elerko secretly helped install another line using the existing infrastructure. This secret line was well-masked. It wasn't connected to the switchboard but to the cable within an outside wall, a place not easy to notice. This phone line was used at certain times and for certain purposes only, and only by these two men. The purpose of the phone was to get themselves help in case of a riot on the island or in case of any major trouble in the country. It was also there for the officer to try to find a better place to work than his current position.

The UDBA member tried through Elerko to achieve some sort of unity of Yugoslav nations amongst the many political prisoners. This made Elerko suspicious to the prisoners. Elerko became more suspicious to other prisoners when he started to repair the officials' equipment. However, he soon started giving us news that would normally take a very long time to reach us, which eventually brought him many followers.

The Blue Angels sensed something was wrong and they watched him closely. As this didn't yield results they gave him a more difficult job, which soon caused him to be ill and he finally had to be admitted to hospital. This happened at the same time as a raging storm. The lightning struck some equipment near the telephone switchboard that also started malfunctioning and needed repair. As there was nobody capable of repairing such a malfunction, a specialist had to be called in from Rijeka. Of course, he soon found something that nobody was expecting. Still, nobody knew who had fitted the secret phone line. The UDBA member from Rijeka was suspected but he wasn't on the island at the time. As soon as he returned to Goli Otok he dug into his work so as not to rouse suspicion. Everybody needed an alibi and everybody had one.

What the prison management realized in the end was a real shock to them, but they had a hard time catching the spy red-handed.

A few weeks later it was time for the UDBA member to be on duty again. He had already planned to take the phone home, but he knew that the circumstances had to be right in order to do so. The phone was now being strictly supervised in order to find out what its real purpose was. He believed that he would have no problem taking it with him, but a UDBA colonel had hired staff to watch and listen to every phone call made on the island. Not even the UDBA was aware of this procedure; the only ones who knew about it were a few trusted men that the colonel had himself chosen.

The UDBA member decided not to take the phone home with him but instead to dump it into the sea. When he thought nobody was watching him he took the phone and was caught immediately. Both he and his engineer were sent away from the island and I never heard any news about them.

"Stjepan, I heard that that Albanian was working in cahoots with the police and now he's gone."

"Serves him right! A traitor of Yugoslavia, he deserves no better. I'd hang them all if it were up to me."

"What do you mean?"

"Here's what I mean. He works to overturn the government and gets nothing out of it. Us thieves, we consume what we steal, and we return it into circulation."

"I'm aware of that. But what you thieves return is less than you take."

"That's true. But what about those that got their war pensions and live on it? Do they give back as much as they take? They don't even know how to disassemble a rifle. They never fought with the Partisans but they all found false witnesses to testify in their favor, and here they are living at the country's expense. So why shouldn't I do the same?"

"I agree with you, Stjepan, but I don't approve of killing men like that Albanian was killed. Anyway, have you heard that the reeducators from the Carpentry and the Concreting made a bet? Apparently the convicts from the Carpentry are better at soccer, but the reeducators from the Concreting won't take it. He says the ones from the Carpentry are better. The winner of the bet wins twenty liters of wine and other drinks. The game's on Sunday, at the big stadium. All convicts are invited to watch."

"We're not working on Sunday then?"

"So it seems. They've apprised the Room Seniors about it. That UDBA guy Radaković is going to be the referee. He's a goalkeeper for the police soccer club so he knows about soccer."

"So, who do you think is going to win?"

"I wouldn't know. How can it be a good game of soccer at all? Exhausted and untrained convicts are supposed to play just because some official wants them to. And they have to play to win."

"That's right, but only those are playing on Sunday who used to play before they came here. Anyway, it's not the result that's important, just as long as we don't have to work on Sunday."

Suddenly Mrki, the policeman, said in his harsh voice: "Why aren't the two of you working? What's with the conversation here?"

"I was just at the toilet, comrade."

"Yeah, but you've been talking here for the last ten minutes. But hey, you'll just report to the commander in the Wires later. I'll tell him you have to do two scrubbings each. Is that clear?"

"Yes, comrade!"

"And what are you waiting for? I said get back to work, both of you!"

*Josip Zoretić*

# Oto

Our shift was over and we reported to the commander in the Wires, but he didn't punish us with scrubbing. Instead we had to carry stones from one heap to another while two other men had to carry them back to the previous heap. They were punished because they didn't take off their hats when their superior from the Carpentry was passing by.

This sort of punishment was only carried out during the night because it was thought to be more effective, both physically and mentally, than if done during the day. And it really was tiresome and nerve-wracking.

Sunday arrived and we really didn't have to work because the game was on. It was a tough match, but without any spectacular moments. It ended in a draw, the result was 2 to 2, so nobody won the bet.

Security measures on the way back from the playground were strict; there was a Blue Angel every twenty meters on both sides of the path. We were counted and sent straight back to the Wires.

"Listen you bastards. If I hear a single word we're not walking to the Wires, you'll have to run! And may snakes bite you if you light up! Get going!" shouted a lieutenant.

He told Lazo, one of the Blue Angels in charge of leading the file, that the file was to start walking. We had to be lined up better than any army file, but this time the file wasn't perfect. The Blue Angels warned us by hitting us with their clubs, and they would as a rule come from behind, unexpectedly. If a convict would react by turning around, he'd get an extra blow, and many convicts were beaten on the way back because the police were angry they had wasted their time at the match.

"Keep to the right," said Lazo from the front of the file of four, and all the other Blue Angels sent the order on. A tractor was coming toward us and the road was too narrow so we had to make way for the tractor to pass us by on the curve near the entrance to the Wires.

"Why did you touch that trailer?" shouted Tomica, an extremely short police officer who stayed with the police after the war.

At the same time the sound of his billy club was heard. He hit Oto Kolenc, a strong Slovene convict.

Tomica grabbed him and knocked him to the ground next to the wall alongside the road. Another Blue Angel came right away to help beat Oto, but Oto took his club away from him and threw it into the rocks and then he grabbed the Blue Angel by his back and behind, lifted him up, and threw him onto the ground. The Blue Angel landed on his hands, but his left hand with a very expensive wristwatch was the first to touch the ground and the watch broke immediately. His ear and face were also injured and general panic broke out. The Blue Angels who came to help out couldn't do much, so they just started beating whomever they could get a hold of.

The convicts from the file ran into the Wires so quickly that they couldn't be counted at the entrance. We were all lucky that we weren't shot at from the nearby watchtowers.

Men ran like hell just to escape the beating.

Blue Angels ordered that the siren be turned on, which was supposed to help get everybody to line up.

None of the Blue Angels even remembered what the person who stood up to them looked like anymore; everybody just wanted to get to Oto.

Whoever was missing from the lineup that followed was considered escaped. They were sure that they weren't going to be able to find out from the convicts who the hero was, at least not in short order.

If Oto had stayed with the rest it could have ended badly for some other men who matched his description, but luckily for the rest, Oto was missing during the counting and the conclusion was that it was him who had caused all the commotion and fought the officers.

While we were being counted, Oto made a plan. He took off his vest, filled it with as many stones as the vest could hold, and climbed the iron tower with the TV antenna. The tower was around forty meters high with pieces of iron welded along it all the way to the top to enable climbing.

The TV tower had to be that high because the convicts' pavilions were in a valley, and the tower couldn't even be seen from farther than five hundred meters away. That is why we could never see the Yugoslav TV program. We only got the Italian one but we weren't allowed to watch it. Only the Blue Angels living near the Quarantine could see the Yugoslav, Italian and Austrian programs. The Blue Angels in the Wires complained because they were deprived the entertainment. The Velebit Mountains were in the way between the Wires and the transmitter, so Zagreb TV, which showed some Yugoslav shows, also couldn't be seen.

Oto was ordered to come down from the tower or he would be shot down, but he persisted. Nobody would shoot him down with so many people watching, he thought to himself –

and he was right.

The lieutenant ordered a Blue Angel to climb up and knock him down if he didn't want to climb down on his own. He only managed to climb halfway up when Oto threw one of his stones and hit him straight in his head. After one more stone thrown his way the Blue Angel had to make his way back down.

"We'll just leave him like that; he won't last long up there. He's going to have to come down eventually."

But wrought-up Angels couldn't resist and ordered the convicts to throw stones at him, which wasn't a very good idea since nobody aimed high enough to hit him. Then someone had an idea that they might try to get him off the tower using water from a fire hose, but the pressure of the sea supply system was too low.

Finally, a commander from the UDBA arrived and ordered the crowd to go away.

"Get down now! That's an order!"

"I'm not coming down because you'll beat the crap out of me if I do."

"I said get down!"

"I'd rather die up here than down there by the hands of your men and dogs."

"I'm giving you my communist word of honor; nobody's going to touch you. You'll get ten days in the solitary and then you're going back to the Wires, and nobody will ever bother you because of this."

Oto then decided to come down and the commander kept his communist word of honor, most likely because if this convict went missing, it couldn't be kept a secret.

He was a real sly dog, that commander. Stories were going around about him being a nice man, and such stories were told mostly by the snitches who had no problem telling the police what they wanted to hear. Very often they'd add lies to their stories just to make themselves seem "reformable" and thus get easier jobs.

The next day we got a communication from the Goli Otok Correctional Institution warden regarding the convicts' insolent attack on the authorities on Sunday. It went as follows:

> I hereby inform you that in case of similar riots the authorities will be allowed to use their weapons to defend themselves and will not be held accountable for the consequences. Every single convict is obliged to obey by the internal regulations. Nobody is allowed to argue with or in any other way oppose the officers. Convicts will continue to live and work as prescribed by the regulations, the Penal Code, and the House Rules of this correctional institution. Even slight disregard of the rules will result in severe punishment in order to reestablish the discipline and restore the previous condition. This is effective immediately.

Reestablishing the discipline was sort of a contradiction in terms. What it involved was allowing the Angels to legally torture the convicts in any way they thought possible. It involved inventing that someone was missing and making us all go out in the rain until we were soaking wet, and sending us back to our beds around midnight. It involved carrying stones that needed no carrying or scrubbing floors that needed no scrubbing – all done at night. It was this that they felt needed restoring; but punishments of this sort were few compared to the number of other forms of punishment.

*Josip Zoretić*

## Savo

"Savo, would you get your machine out of the way, my men need to pass by."

And Savo gave the order: "Two steps back everyone!"

A tired man from the town of Split didn't hear the order right away because he had spent most of the night scrubbing and didn't go to sleep until 2 a.m. He was practically sleeping on his feet while Savo Grahovac was counting the convicts. The aggressive Savo kicked the man from Split between the legs and the man collapsed and started to squirm in agony.

"Take that piece of scum to the Center to see the lieutenant. I'll be there shortly," said Savo, pointing at two convicts that had to take him away

They lifted him up but he couldn't stand on his own so they carried him to the Center by holding him under his armpits. He was punished with three days in the solitary because he didn't step back in time. In the solitary he was beaten over and over again, but he was lucky that his genitals, although severely beaten, stayed in place. The doctor allowed him to spend ten days in the hospital solitary where he had some time to recuperate.

Such difficult living conditions continuously forced men to think about ways to escape from the island, but they rarely succeeded.

*Goli Otok*

## Stevo

One day a dark-complexioned young man came to me at work and said, "Listen, buddy, hope you don't mind my asking, where are you from?"

When I answered the question, another one followed. "How much time do you still have to serve here?"

"Quite a lot and I don't know how I'll make it. You know what it's like here. I don't think I can make my way out of here alive."

"I don't think I'm in a better situation than you. But listen, a friend of yours, H. from Rijeka, told me a little about you. He's a friend of mine as well. I'd like to ask you something, so if you're willing to tell me . . . "

"Listen, buddy, I don't know you."

"I know you're scared. It's not surprising. But don't be, I'm not one of those snitches. My name's Stevo Mađarević, from Vinkovci. I'm sure you've heard of my case. My lover and I killed her husband. He was a lousy husband, no good, so I made love to her secretly. But we couldn't take it anymore and we decided to take him out. It was all discovered soon, so she got twelve years and I got thirteen. She's in jail in Požega and I'm here. I doubt I could last here that many years. I came to the conclusion that I have to get out of here, and abroad is where I plan to go. Do you know if there's a country that doesn't extradite murderers?"

"Sure, there's France, but you'd have to join the Foreign Legion. I can't really give you the information you need because I don't know much. And as I said, I don't know you."

"Can you please think about it? You'll see I'm

not a snitch."

I didn't feel like talking to him because to me he didn't seem like a nice person. I was simply sick when I remembered he took a life in order to have a good time with somebody else's wife when there were so many other options. And it wasn't easy to confide in others on the island. It wasn't uncommon for a person you thought to be your best friend to report you to the officials.

After a while Stevo was doing the afternoon shift and this gave him more chances to run away because the murderers weren't watched as closely as the rest of us.

I heard he was a good swimmer and still he was found dead, floating on the sea surface, wearing a life jacket. I'll let the reader think about how he managed to drown.

After he was found dead – which was yet another case the Blue Angels used as an intimidation technique that was supposed to make the convicts think twice before attempting an escape – many made comments such as "he's better off that way, at least his suffering has stopped now."

*Goli Otok*

# Makoli

Difficult jobs carried out by the C category convicts in the Quarry and the B category in the Wires forced people to commit various types of sabotages – the hatred toward the state increased daily. Enemies of the state grew in number and they came from all parts of Yugoslavia.

It wouldn't be fair to say that all the inhuman procedures that happened on Goli Otok were a product of Tito's mind, but the lives of the convicts on the island didn't change much even after Ranković was relieved and the warden replaced in 1966.

The warden was involved in the preparations for creating Greater Serbia, along with Ranković and others. He had taken 75 million dinars from the prison treasury to buy weapons abroad, and to pay the police forces that were being created by Ranković to carry out a coup and remove Tito from the head of state. This was later discovered and the warden was replaced, but he didn't stay on the island as a prisoner. A new warden arrived but the laws stayed the same. It seems proof enough that Tito knew about what was going on on Goli Otok.

On a hot day in 1967 a 300-meter file was at the gate to the Wires on the way from work. The guards were being relieved and a fresh lot counted us. The Blue Angels that were on duty counted us again upon our entrance into the Wires. Now we had to transform the file of four into a file of two, which was now doubly long and formed a circle. And so we waited for lunch – spaghetti and sauerkraut mixed together.

One of the Blue Angels went to check the

back of the file and everybody was waiting for his sign before they could start handing out lunch. A police officer was waiting for the sign by the cauldron, but Malić gave the order that the back of the file should get food first.

"A" category convicts were at the front, and some of them rushed to the back. They all had easier jobs, wore better suits, and were never supervised. Generally they were better off than the rest and felt they were entitled to be among the first to get their food. No sooner than they started going to the back did the Blue Angels ruthlessly start beating them and anyone they ran into. Men left the file and ran off, and the A category convicts started shouting that nobody should get lunch that day.

The chaos lasted for about ten minutes before a siren was heard, which meant that we were all to line up again. Then a major asked: "Why don't you want to eat?"

"We just won't."

"Fine, you don't have to eat if you don't want to. But you all do have to obey by the House Rules."

While he was talking we could see armed Blue Angels lying around in the rocks, trained dogs with them. There were no new riots because the "better" convicts went back on their decision and started moving toward the cauldron.

It was Azem Makoli who ended up getting in trouble because of this – a man who had already been seriously tortured more than once. He was one of the first to finish lunch that day and was headed for the gate, carrying some books in his hands.

Whoever was illiterate or couldn't speak Serbo-Croatian had to go to school or learn a trade if he was sentenced to many years on Goli

*Goli Otok*

Otok. Only a small number of trades were taught, and it was all theory and no practice. If you already knew a trade you weren't allowed to learn a new one because that would mean less time to do the jobs suited for mental and physical tormenting of the anti-state items.

Makoli approached the gate where maddened Angels and their dogs were waiting for him.

"Just where do you think you're going?"

"To school, comrade. The file always gathers outside the dormitory and leaves from there. Since lunch was late today I thought I was late too, and I don't like being late."

"And have you informed the officials you were going to the gate?"

"No, comrade."

"Well, well. So you think you can just do whatever you like, do you?"

"No, commander, I've made a mistake and I'm sorry. I won't do it again."

The big and strong Radaković didn't use his billy club but slapped him with the back of one hand and then hit him in the stomach with the other one. Makoli was on the ground within a second.

Nearby was a dog trainer with two German shepherds. He brought them to the gate to help catch convicts in case of a riot or an attempted escape. He wasn't holding them very tightly and when the dogs saw Makoli on the ground they got loose, or the dog trainer loosened the leash on purpose. The dogs were all over Makoli, biting him where they could, which was easy considering he was wearing only shorts and a short-sleeved blouse, like all B and C category convicts did. During this time the brave police officer was continually kicking him.

You couldn't tell what was more painful – the

biting or the kicking. The dogs destroyed his legs. The kicking damaged his ribs.

At this moment the file heading for school came along but Makoli was in no condition to walk anymore, so we lifted him up and carried him to the dormitory. There was blood all over him and all we could do was bandage him with some bed sheets and try to stop him from bleeding to death.

Blood was still coming out through several layers of our improvised bandage. The bleeding eventually stopped and the wound curdled. Now we were afraid he might get sepsis because of all the bite wounds.

We decided to take the chance and ask a police lieutenant to let us take him to the doctor. He had already heard of what had happened and wanted to make sure the doctor was really necessary. Once he saw how blue Makoli's legs were he allowed the four of us to place him on a stretcher and carry him to the hospital which was over half a kilometer away from the Wires.

He then informed the assistant warden, Radoslav Runko, about the case, but he only allowed the doctor to give Makoli an anti-tetanus shot and ordered that Makoli be returned to the Wires because the police reported him to have attempted to escape through the gate, where the dogs allegedly stopped him. Runko believed it and watched Makoli leave the hospital in excruciating pain.

The lieutenant thought Makoli was going to die and he didn't want it to happen in front of other convicts, so he asked the assistant warden to allow Makoli to be admitted to hospital again. This was granted under the condition that Makoli give a written request saying he had been touching the dogs and it was that that triggered the unlucky event, and asking the warden to forgive him and grant him the medical care he needed to save his life. The petition was to be handwritten and signed personally. As Makoli was in no condition to write, one of his colleagues wrote it for him.

He survived, but his entire body was full of scars from the bite wounds.

Since he still had a lot of time to serve and never wanted to be the kind of man the police wanted him to be, he was seriously hurt on several occasions. He will forever have vivid memories of Blue Angels on the island, as will many others that survived the hell of the prison on Goli Otok.

\*\*\*

During the last few years I spent on the island, word about what was happening on Goli Otok was making its way around the country. It greatly affected the authorities because they met with great resistance among the people, especially after the case when two of the Blue Angels from the island had to take care of some personal business in Zagreb. They couldn't manage to keep a low profile – they got beaten on their first day in the city and didn't know by whom and ended up spending a long time in a Zagreb hospital. What the Goli Otok authorities were doing to us resulted in their leaving the island and going to any town in Yugoslavia turning into a great risk to their lives.

*Josip Zoretić*

# Kadić

One night three masked men in civilian clothes came to the prison kitchen carrying guns. A man named Kadić was among them. A Hungarian man and some other men were working the night shift. The Hungarian was in charge of food preparation and overseeing the work of his staff, also watching for possible escape attempts. The kitchen was situated practically on the beach, very close to the bay surrounded by the rocks, and it offered a slight chance of escaping.

Kadić came to the island landing in that very bay. He had already spent some time on Goli Otok for not wanting to serve in the army. After leaving the island the muscular young man made his way to West Germany, where he met two well-off brothers whose sister had been killed by a man named Stojan because she refused to marry him. They didn't conform with the fact that Stojan was sentenced to fifteen years in prison. They thought it more suitable to try the man themselves.

Kadić knew his way around the island and knew that Stojan was working and sleeping in the kitchen, so the brothers bought a speedboat and gathered reward money for Kadić if they managed to capture Stojan.

The three of them broke into the kitchen building when there were no police officers there. It was a time when everybody was asleep, so no special security measures were necessary within the Wires.

Kadić turned off the boat motors and rowed the boat along the rocks all the way to the kitchen building. One of the brothers stayed outside to keep guard and the other two entered and asked the Hungarian man about Stojan's whereabouts. Stojan was luckily in hospital because of some eye problems, but Kadić knew the Hungarian guy well; he knew he was a friend of the police so he didn't believe him. When he pointed the gun at others, they corroborated their boss's statement.

Looking for Stojan in the hospital would involve appearing at a lit-up spot with a police watch nearby, so that was out of the question. The three men had to leave the island without having done what they had planned.

The Hungarian cook once again proved his allegiance – he ran out of the kitchen and notified the police as soon as the three intruders left. The phones started ringing, the police were alarmed, the weapons were out. The guard on duty had noticed a speedboat but he believed it to be one of the island police's boats patrolling around the island. After he received a phone call he started shooting with his machine gun but the night impaired his vision and he couldn't make a shot so far away. The police speedboat was probably better and faster than theirs, but the crew that was to follow the intruders was told the intruders were armed. As nobody knew exactly what kind of arms they had on them, the police refused to go after them but instead decided to ask the Navy for help. It didn't occur to them that the intruders' mission was getting Stojan, but one of many prisoners with long-term sentences. The cooks couldn't see their faces and didn't know who their leader was.

Everyone was on high alert; the clerks and orderlies later told us that for a few days the officers never put down their arms, not even when they went to the bathroom or in the rooms to which only the police and reformed convicts had access to, the latter being imprisoned because they never wanted to lay their hands on guns.

Kadić directed his boat toward the Slovenian coast and there the men split up – Kadić went to Ljubljana and the other two to Italy. The Navy held the island surrounded for a week, but all was in vain – the intruders were not to be found.

Entire Yugoslavia was notified and control was strict at all border crossings, but Kadić was prepared for everything. Not only did he carry firearms, he also had a gas gun hidden in his sock.

He was originally from Bosnia and a large number of Bosnians were working in Ljubljana. Some of them were his acquaintances and former neighbors. He took one of his Bosnian neighbors with him, put him in a car he had previously stolen and headed straight for the Austrian border. When they were near the town of Celje the traffic police noticed them when they were speeding. They were even more suspicious because they wore imported suits.

Suddenly the rotation light of the police car was on and they were supposed to stop. Kadić was a good driver and even though he was driving a car he didn't know well he decided to speed up even more. After half an hour of chase on unknown roads the police car won.

"Why were you running away? May I see your driver's license, please?"

As there was no answer, the police officers handcuffed them and radioed to their superiors they had apprehended some car thieves and needed no backup. They decided to take the stolen car to Ljubljana with the thieves in it, and off they were.

When they entered a village the driver of the civilian car decided to stop at a local shop and buy himself a soda because he was very thirsty, and his colleague had no problems with it.

Kadić knew what would happen to him if the police found out what he had done, so he took advantage of the opportunity.

The police officers never checked his socks. His hands were cuffed at the front so he took out the gun and shot the officer that remained in the car, then sat on the driver's seat and stepped on the gas. After a few hundred meters he stopped and threw the police officer out of the car, took away his keys and uncuffed himself. The officer that had stepped out of the car also had to go to the bathroom so Kadić had time.

Kadić continued to drive toward the Austrian border without any problems. When he was near the border he left the car by the side of the road and continued on foot, successfully crossing the border.

I learned of this when I met him in the West-German town of Fürth after I was released from prison.

*Josip Zoretić*

# Almost There

I have to admit I was rather pessimistic when I first started serving my sentence. I was sure I wouldn't be able to survive the things around me, the things I saw and suffered myself. I thought no human being could. But I was wrong. Human beings are tougher than they seem. I saw traces of hope every time I saw someone leave the island.

Of course, serving sentences on Goli Otok left marks on people's bodies for life and there is not one person who can say he hasn't been beaten at least once. The island took its toll on me as well, but I don't wish to relate them, no matter how serious they are. That is something I intend to take with me to my grave.

"Sadist State" would've been a fitting name for the island. The authorities did whatever they felt like doing to people who couldn't do anything about it.

The legislation published in the Yugoslav press didn't really exist, and not all nationalities were really equal. Albanians were most horribly treated. The statute concerning imprisonment says clearly that prisoners mustn't be beaten. But if you mentioned that to a commander that beat you, you'd get an answer like this one: 'You don't understand anything. It's not the law that I'm beating up; it's you, your back. The law is out there somewhere, locked in a drawer, and you don't know anything about it.'

There was absolutely nothing we could do about it because they did whatever they pleased. They never had to explain why and how people went missing.

A day one didn't get beaten up was a good

day.

When my seven long years on the island were coming to an end I became optimistic. I started to believe my foot would touch the mainland again. The joy I felt was increasing day in and day out.

I was now allowed to receive some money from my brother in Australia, but before that I had to discuss it with one of the reeducators. One of the first things he said to me was: "I don't think this sentence of yours has served its purpose and I honestly hope you come here again some day. Well, maybe not exactly here since you're too old . . . Now you've got ninety days left and you wish to write to your brother and ask him for money. You do that, but I don't want you mentioning one word about what it's like here, got that? You see, I read every letter before it leaves the island."

My brother sent me a letter with a one hundred Australian dollar check. When it arrived the officer read it and made a red note on the envelope: 'You have received a check of one hundred dollars. The money has been converted to British pounds and is kept in the treasury.' And then he signed it.

Days were going by and nobody paid much attention to me anymore. The days became longer but they weren't difficult.

*Josip Zoretić*

# The Last Day

July 9, 1969 arrived, the day I left Goli Otok. I became so detached from the outside world that I could hardly believe I was going to be in it soon.

Some other men were leaving Goli Otok that same day. At around 8:00 an officer arrived and sent us to the repository to return the suits and other equipment. If you didn't return the things issued, you'd have to pay for it before getting your civilian clothes back, but this was not the case in our group.

Afternoon came and we were on the dock, waiting for release certificates that proved we had served our sentences to the end, and for the money from the Dead Fund. Since we were still alive they had to give it to us, and we had to wait for half an hour. It was brought to us in envelopes and we had to sign for it. When it was my turn to sign I first wanted to read what the paper said and I wanted the officer to count the money in front of me. He felt offended by my request, so he just threw all the money on the desk. Another officer read the form and said everything was in order, so I asked, "What do you mean, everything is in order? My check's not here; where is it?"

"What check? I don't know what you're talking about. Do you have the receipt saying you received a check?"

"No, I don't have it."

"Then sign the paper and shut the hell up!"

I had thrown away the letter with the clerk's signature so any form of argument was risky for me, but I still refused to sign.

Then he started threatening: "I'll send you back to the Quarry, you know, I have the authority to do that!"

*Goli Otok*

But he knew he didn't, and he knew he wasn't allowed to hit me because I'd leave Goli Otok with fresh wounds. I started calling him a liar, a thief, and all the names I could think of and he raised his hand to hit me, but another officer stopped him. He then rushed to telephone the lieutenant and asked to lock me up again, but this didn't intimidate me either. I continued the argument with the lieutenant and this man somehow got the impression I was telling the truth. He called the clerk that would clear things up. After two hours waiting I got my check and an apology; apparently the check had been misplaced.

Just before I left the island I witnessed another terrible scene. A man was lying on the shore, groaning with pain because both of his legs were broken. He had been carrying an immense amount of rocks, slipped and fell over. The rocks he was carrying landed on his legs and broke them.

I asked the commanding officer, "Couldn't you place something underneath him? Look at him, he's lying on the rocky ground and he's in pain."

"It won't hurt him to stay like that. As far as I'm concerned he can die. Who asked him to come here anyway? And he can run away from here too, there's nobody watching him." And he started laughing ironically.

Now that this was done we started boarding the Cer. We were searched for hidden messages or any papers that might compromise the authorities on Goli Otok. As nothing of the sort was found on any of us, the boat sailed off toward Jurjevo, a small town at the foot of Velebit, just a little to the south of Senj, in the direction of Split.

It was windy so the boat was rocking, and a young man from Smederevo was lying on the deck, in pain, large water drops brought by the wind falling all over him. I later learned his name was Predrag. One of the civilians who was leaving the island as well, I didn't know his name, approached the commanding officer that escorted us and asked if he should lift him up and carry him inside the boat.

"Why?" the commander asked. "You're a civilian and you should know civilians aren't allowed to talk to convicted men."

Nobody was to interfere with the inhuman treatment, but we continued to nag, at which he reacted, "It's not the first time you've seen a hurt man. He'll be alright."

The boat finally landed and the crew carried him out and placed him on a bench. One of the Angels told him, "I've called Rijeka and notified them we're here. The ambulance will be here shortly to take you to the hospital."

The first bus to Rijeka was crowded so we had to wait for the next one.

The officer left Predrag on the bench and went to have a drink in a bar, watching him closely through the window. We came close to Predrag and asked him if he was in pain, although we knew he was, and asked him if he had a cigarette. Of course he didn't, and he was longing for one, but the trouble was, we weren't allowed to buy him any or he would get in trouble. Still, he decided to let us buy him some.

The officer had gone to the bar just to get away from us, sensing we were hostile to him; so we went inside and asked him in front of many witnesses if he allowed us to buy some cigarettes for Predrag. He said it was alright. If his answer had been negative we would have beaten him up. We bought ten packs and gave them to Predrag. Twenty minutes later our bus arrived and took us to Rijeka, and Predrag stayed in Jurjevo waiting for his ambulance. That was the last time we saw him.

*Josip Zoretić*

# Final Escape

I arrived at Ljubljana and started looking for a job, but wherever I applied I was asked where I had worked before and why I had quit. It wasn't bad until they heard I was a former convict. In many companies they hadn't even heard of the island of Goli, let alone about the prison there. I couldn't lie because working on Goli Otok wasn't considered working and wasn't registered as such. Whenever I explained how I had spent my years I would get answers like, "I'm sorry but we don't need anyone at the moment. Maybe some other time."

After Ljubljana I went to Zagreb, but Goli Otok was quite a known term there. Again I was asked what I had been doing up to then. I gave the same answers and got the same replies as in Ljubljana. I couldn't conform with it so I went to Belgrade, but things were even worse there.

Hopeless, I tried to complain but could never get past the doorman in the Federal Executive Committee building, the highest executive body in Yugoslavia, just below the president of the state. I was thrown out very quickly – two civilian officers were kind to me until I told them whom I needed to see and why. Then they told me to follow the regular procedure, opened the door and kicked me out.

Not even after two months of looking could I find proper employment. I did odd jobs in various private companies, but that was illegal – I wasn't paying taxes and I ran the risk of being reported, arrested, and sent back to prison. This was not how I saw my future and it seemed there was no future for me in Yugoslavia at all.

When I left the island I was told to report to

the local police and the town hall once I decided where I was going to live, which I did as soon as I arrived at Belgrade. The clerk there told me I had to call every three days and inform them about what I was doing or if I was going somewhere so that they could notify the local police I was arriving. I didn't take it seriously, but after a while I received to my apartment address a writ saying I had to report about my moves.

I realized there was no hope for me in Yugoslavia so I decided once again to leave the country.

I heard that there was a Serbian lady who worked at a travel agency in Karlovac who was friendly to Croats, so I though I would try and get a passport through her. I told her I wanted to go to France to visit my aunt and that I would be back in two weeks. She told me to come back with two pictures, but I was prepared and already had them with me. Two hours later I had a passport.

The next day my mother roasted two chickens for me and I ate one of them. I said good-bye for the last time and used the one hundred dollars that my brother sent me to buy a train ticket to Austria. I took my chances and never thought about what might become of me if things didn't work out for me abroad. I was lucky that West Germany offered me much more than I was expecting; I got a decent job and a decent salary.

Everything that happened on Goli Otok was kept a secret; even survivors don't talk about the atrocities committed because they are very hard to believe. The worst things that happened haven't even been described. But they did happen, and there are thousands of witnesses that would say I left so much out and that it was much worse than what I wrote. But this is exactly why I left out so many things – because I would like for this book to someday get to the hands of some of the butchers whose names I have mentioned, and they will have to admit that I kept the worst part to myself and have acted more justly to them than they have to those that didn't fit their regime.

After many years of suffering I managed to shake off the yoke of the Yugoslav regime and its empty promises given to me and to millions of others. I heard many different opinions about Yugoslavia and came to the conclusion that it was best that I went as far away as possible and forget the wrongs that were done to me. I've been trying. Here I am in Canada, far from my torture chamber, trying to forget. But as people say, bad things aren't forgotten easily.

Josip Zoretić

*Goli Otok*

Located in Sošice, Croatia, the sign indicates the mound of bones ("kosturi") in the deep cavern where my father and many others lie.

The memorial at the site of the mass grave in Sošice.

Today this sign greets visitors to Goli Otok.

## Goli Otok

The sign on the "stolarija" building, where mostly chairs were made, reads "Živeo Drug Tito" – Long Live Comrade Tito.

Bodies were buried on the hill behind the prison buildings. The upper floor of the building in the back was not completed until after I left in 1969.

The reservoir was used to collect rain water. Bodies were buried in the area between the reservoir and the power substation in the distance.

*Goli Otok*

My release paper.

*Josip Zoretić*

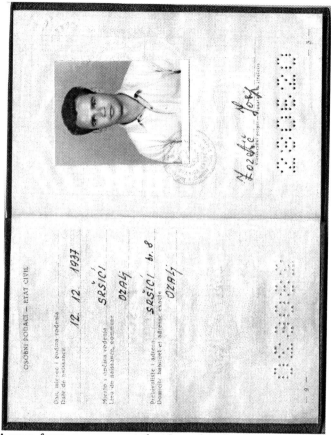

A page from my passport that I used to finally escape from Yugoslavia in 1969.

CPSIA information can be obtained at www.ICGtesting.com
Printed in the USA
240822LV00001B/37/A